P9-CCY-096

THE DEVIL'S HORSEMEN

The Devil's Horsemen

THE MONGOL INVASION OF EUROPE

James Chambers

ATHENEUM   NEW YORK
1979

Library of Congress Cataloging in Publication Data

Chambers, James.
    The Devil's horsemen.

        1. Mongols—History.   2. Europe—History—476–1492.
3. Military art and science—History.   4. Military
history, Medieval.   5. Church history—Middle Ages, 600–
1500.   I. Title.
DS19.C45   1979   909'.04'94202   78–22055
ISBN 0–689–10942–3

Contents

Illustrations

Maps

Preface

SEVERAL books have been written in English about the Mongol conquests, the subsequent empires which the Mongols ruled, the travellers who visited them and even the diplomatic relations between their khans and the papacy. But nothing has been written about the Mongol invasion of Europe. In this book I have rashly endeavoured to fill that gap. But I did not set out to write a detailed account of every event that took place in Europe during the invasion. I have simply attempted to tell the story of an extraordinary campaign, outline its causes and far-reaching consequences and place it in its historical perspective.

The contemporary sources were written in more than ten languages and it is unlikely that anyone could read them all in their original. Fortunately, however, most of the Middle Eastern and Oriental sources have been translated into at least one European language by eminent scholars who have added their own notes and commentaries. These translations are listed in the Bibliography and their notes and commentaries were often my guides when the Latin sources were contradictory and the bias of modern Central European historians was obvious. I must also acknowledge that I could not have found my way through the maze of contemporary sources without the further guidance of the leading histories of the Mongol period, particularly the works of G. Vernadsky, B. Spuler, I. de Rachewiltz and J.J. Saunders, and above all the notes and articles of P. Pelliot.

There are now many ways of spelling Mongol names. In the past Europeans based their transliteration on Arabic. Thus, for example, since there is no 'ch' in Arabic, Chingis Khan was spelt Jingis Khan and then Genghis Khan. But today it is more common to present the names in a form that is closer to their Oriental pronunciation and this I have attempted to do. However, I have also tried to spell them in a way which will be easy to read and where the Oriental form is very different from the older European spelling, I have only adapted the older form to bring it closer to the Oriental without making it unrecognizable.

Finally I would like to thank Sheila Murphy for her encouragement, Christopher Falkus for his infectious enthusiasm and confidence, my editor, Christine Sandeman, for her patience and judgement, and my wife Josephine for her tolerance.

London 1978   *James Chambers*

To Josephine

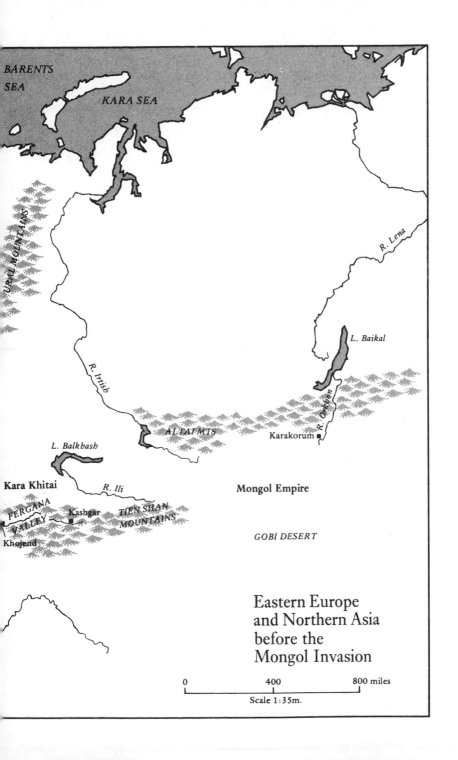

BARENTS
SEA

KARA SEA

URAL MOUNTAINS

R. Lena

L. Baikal

R. Irtish

R. Orkhon

ALTAI MTS

Karakorum

L. Balkhash

Kara Khitai

R. Ili

Mongol Empire

FERGANA
VALLEY

Kashgar

TIEN SHAN
MOUNTAINS

Khojend

GOBI DESERT

Eastern Europe
and Northern Asia
before the
Mongol Invasion

0   400   800 miles

Scale 1:35m.

1
The First Move West

IN the late winter of 1220, Ali ad-Din boarded the only remaining fishing boat in the village of Astara on the shores of the Caspian Sea and sailed out towards the island of Abeskum.

As he passed through the village dressed in rags, he and his handful of followers appeared to be nothing more than another group of refugees, but a few months before Ali ad-Din had been Muhammad Ali Shah, Emperor of Khwarizm, Transoxiana and Khurasan. His rich empire had stretched from the Persian Gulf and the Caspian Sea to the river Indus and the Hindu Kush, yet in those few months he had lost it all; and as the boat pulled away the shore behind became thick with mounted archers charging hopelessly into the water, their arrows falling short in its wake.

When he came to the throne of Khwarizm in 1200 as Muhammad II, Ali ad-Din also inherited the enormous army with which he had already begun the easy conquest of Khurasan. His empire had been founded by Khutbeddin Muhammad, a Turkish mercenary who had governed the area on behalf of the Seljuks and acquired enough wealth and power to declare independence. Although the indigenous population was Persian, Muhammad II's courtiers and soldiers were the Turkish descendants of Khutbeddin's mercenaries, and the fierce corps of horsemen who formed his bodyguard were Kanglis, a tribe of Kipchaks or eastern Cumans from the steppes beyond the Aral Sea, imported by his mother Turkan Khatun, who was the daughter of their chief. Against such soldiers as these the peaceful Persian people of Khurasan could offer no more than token resistance.

Although he was ambitious, Muhammad was irresolute and un-imaginative. He bolstered his lack of security with the strength of his army and camouflaged his lack of confidence with vanity. The easy conquest of his ill-defended neighbours offered him the opportunity not only to indulge an army that was too large to justify in time of peace, but also to increase his own wealth and enhance his reputation. Continuing the campaign that he had begun under his father, he led his army through the rich, irrigated farm lands that had once been desert, secured the ancient cities and annexed the whole of Khurasan to his empire. The operation took not much longer than the time required for his army to cover the distance, but it brought him the prestige that he longed for. While he proclaimed himself to the world as 'the chosen prince of Allah' and his sycophantic courtiers nicknamed him the second Alexander, his neighbours, fearful of his army and his ambition, began to offer him tribute and allegiance.

To the east of Muhammad's empire lay the empire of Transoxiana and to the north-east of that, the powerful Buddhist empire of Kara Khitai, which bordered the eastern steppes and screened the kingdoms of Islam from the new empire of the nomad Mongols. When Muhammad, 'the chosen prince of Allah', refused to pay any further tribute to the infidel rulers of Kara Khitai, Osman, Emperor of Transoxiana, transferred his own allegiance from Kara Khitai to Khwarizm. Both Osman and Muhammad believed that internal struggles would prevent the Buddhist army from protecting its interests, but when Kara Khitai was invaded from the east by the Mongols, Muhammad saw the chance that even his caution could not resist. While Kara Khitai fell to the Mongols the Khwarizmian army marched almost unopposed into Transoxiana. By opportunism, and without ever really testing his army in the field, Muhammad had made himself one of the most powerful rulers in Islam and with the revenues of Transoxiana in his coffers he was unquestionably the richest.

Lying between the Amu Darya and the Syr Darya, rivers which were known in the west as the Oxus and the Jaxartes, desolated in the north by the impenetrable desert of Kizil Kum and only made fertile in the south by extensive irrigation, Transoxiana was not rich in natural resources, but across its heart ran the overland trade routes of the world. At the eastern end of the road on the Syr Darya stood the commercial centre of Khojend, in the west near the Amu Darya the mosques, universities and carpet warehouses of Bukhara and between them the city that Muhammad II had chosen for his new capital, Samarkand.

Huge suburbs shaded by poplar trees and decorated with

fountains and canals surrounded a city so rich that even within its walls every house had a garden. In the factories the citizens wove silk, cotton and silver lamé, the Persian craftsmen worked saddles, harnesses and decorated copper and the workshops of the Chinese quarter produced the rag paper that was used throughout the Middle East. From the fields beyond the suburbs the farmers exported melons and aubergines wrapped in snow and packed in lead boxes. The vast population exceeded five hundred thousand. It was in Samarkand that Muhammad's courtiers housed their treasures and their harems and lived in a splendour that was unequalled even in the east; it was from there that they rode out to hunt dressed in cloth of gold with tame cheetahs clinging on to the saddles behind them.

Muhammad settled down to enjoy the magnificence of his new capital, but he did not disband his army. An avaricious tax collector, he was as unpopular among the Persian inhabitants of his huge empire as were his plundering Turkish soldiers. To allay his fears of rebellion the army had to be kept at full strength and to keep that army contented and maintain his reputation as a conqueror he would occasionally lead it out on minor expeditions against neighbouring cities in the south. Muhammad Shah's Persian subjects were, however, helpless. They could turn only to their religious leaders, but these were engaged in a series of sectarian quarrels, and Nasir, Caliph of Baghdad, and spiritual ruler of Islam, had neither the temporal power nor the unity to offer anything more than a desultory chain of hopeless intrigues.

It was after his siege of Ghazna in 1216 that Muhammad first learned of these intrigues. The threat was insignificant, but Muhammad was a timid man. He determined to depose the caliph and replace him with a puppet. Receiving the submission of Azerbaijan and Fars which lay along his route, he marched his army towards Baghdad. It was as though the Holy Roman Emperor were to lead an army towards the gates of Rome. But if the caliph was powerless, Allah was not. The army was dispersed in the mountains by a fierce snowstorm and many of those who did not die of exposure had their throats cut by Kurdish bandits. Muhammad was forced to withdraw, and for the time being, the caliph survived.

Returning to Bukhara the shah found three ambassadors waiting for him. They were men of Khwarizmian origin who had been

living in Kara Khitai and they carried gifts so precious that even
the shah was impressed: gold ingots and a huge gold nugget, jade
and ivory ornaments and cloaks spun from the wool of white
camels. When they had laid these before him they delivered a
letter.

I send you these gifts. I know your power and the vast extent of your
empire and I regard you as my most cherished son. For your part you
must know that I have conquered China and all the Turkish nations
north of it; my country is an anthill of soldiers and a mine of silver and I
have no need of other lands. Therefore I believe that we have an equal
interest in encouraging trade between our subjects.

Beneath the letter was a seal and on it inscribed, 'God in heaven,
the Kah Khan, the power of God on Earth. The Seal of the
Emperor of Mankind.'

That evening the shah dined with the ambassadors. If the un-
concluded feud with the caliph and the depletion of his army had
not embarrassed the 'chosen prince of Allah' with more insecurity
than he could tolerate, he might well have treated the infidel
barbarians with the contempt that they deserved. He knew very
little about the Mongol conquerors from the east, although self-
interest had made him send messages of good will during the
invasion of Kara Khitai, but if the khan could be trusted the
advantages of a trade agreement were obvious. He questioned his
guests, asking if the 'Emperor of Mankind' was really as powerful
as his letter claimed, and the ambassadors, forewarned of his
vanity, replied tactfully that although powerful, he was not as
powerful as the shah; and they answered honestly when they said
that he did not have as many soldiers.

Muhammad seemed satisfied by the flattery and by 1218 a
commercial treaty had been signed. Khwarizmian trade with the
east could now continue unaltered by the spread of Mongol rule
and protected by an alliance too powerful to be challenged.

The Caliph of Baghdad, growing hysterical as he watched the
shah's army regaining its strength, decided to make one last effort
to save his neck and sent a secret messenger to the Mongol khan
pleading for his intervention and warning him not to trust the
ambitious shah. So elaborate were his precautions that the message
was tattooed on to the envoy's shaved head and he was not allowed
to set out until the hair had grown again. But the effort was wasted.
At the Mongol capital of Karakorum the messenger was told that

the khan was at peace with the shah and he was sent home without an audience.

Soon after the treaty was signed the first Mongol caravan arrived at Otrar beyond the Syr Darya, led by three Moslem merchants and accompanied by a Mongol ambassador, commissioned to buy the luxurious products of Transoxiana for the nobles at the Mongol court. The shah, who had not heard how the khan had treated the caliph's messenger, still doubted his reliability and when he received a letter from Inalchuk Khwadir Khan, the governor of Otrar, reporting his suspicions that these merchants were spies, he ordered that if the case could be proved the men were to be put to death. It is possible that the merchants were spies, since all Mongol merchants were expected to make military reports wherever necessary, but it is unlikely, since Otrar was so near to the border that the Mongols must have known everything about it already. In either event the suspicion was insignificant enough to warrant no more than a complaint, but the five hundred camels laden with gold, silver, silk and sables were too much of a temptation for the rapacious governor. Without an investigation or a trial he murdered the ambassador, the merchants and the men who led their camels and confiscated their property.

The governor had exceeded his authority and Muhammad could easily have placated the inevitable Mongol outrage by expressing his own abhorrence of the crime and punishing the culprit, but when Ibn Kafraj Boghra arrived at Samarkand as an ambassador from one ally to another, escorted only by two Mongol soldiers and demanding merely that the murderer should be tried and punished, the shah burned the beards and hair of the escorts and gave them Boghra's severed head to carry back to Karakorum.

It is difficult to see what the shah hoped to gain by such apparently calculated arrogance. Certainly he was ashamed that the richest prince in Islam had been obliged by temporary weakness to make a treaty with an infidel, but the result of his treachery and insults was bound to be a declaration of war. Muhammad had never been a diplomat, he had assumed his reputation as a conqueror and it would seem that he had begun to believe his own publicity. His army was stronger than ever now; he had four hundred thousand men in Transoxiana alone, twice as many as the Mongols had ever managed to raise. Perhaps he believed that he could control the trade routes to the east himself, or perhaps he saw this as another opportunity to enhance his reputation by fighting a defensive war on his own ground with vastly superior numbers and prove himself the only man on earth capable of defeating 'The Emperor of Mankind', Chingis Khan. Whatever his motive, the outcome was disaster. Mobilizing for the last time what was the most effective army in the world, the Mongol khan turned it towards the west. For the rest of his life and the life of his successor it was never to be disbanded.

Temujin, Chingis Khan, had retired alone to the haunted shores of Lake Baikal in the grim mountains of northern Mongolia. With the exception of his ten thousand strong imperial guard, the garrisons in conquered kingdoms and one expedition in China, his soldiers had been sent home to their tribes. Satisfied with the size of his empire and always in awe of the civilizations that surrounded him, he had begun to live like them through trade and diplomacy, but the paranoia that had influenced his early life was returning and his love of war was never satisfied. The generosity and loyalty for which he was justly respected in the east had been met in the west with contempt. 'The greatest pleasure,' he had said, 'is to vanquish your enemies and chase them before you, to rob them of their wealth and see those dear to them bathed in tears, to ride their horses and clasp to your bosom their wives and daughters.' From now on his policy would be that his empire should never be bounded by a kingdom strong enough to threaten its security. Mongol tradition demanded that the murder of the ambassadors should be avenged and if there was to be a war of attrition it might as well be also a war of conquest.

Returning to his city of tents at Karakorum, Chingis Khan summoned his nation of soldiers and sent one last message to the shah: 'You have chosen war. That will happen which will happen and what it is to be we know not; only God knows.'

In Transoxiana the magnificent army of Muhammad Shah waited for the Mongols to advance. Four hundred thousand Khwarizmian Turks and Persian auxiliaries as well as thousands more armed slaves were drawn up in a cordon along five hundred miles of the Syr Darya, with lines of communication stretching back through the garrisoned cities of Khojend, Samarkand and Bukhara into Khwarizm and Khurasan. Mounted on thoroughbred horses and armed with decorated helmets, burnished shields and steel blades that had been bent to the hilt in the forges, the

Khwarizmian cavalry lived in luxurious camps that were served by trains of camels and elephants, but much of the rest of the army was inexperienced and ill-disciplined and morale was low. The Persian civilians were not entirely opposed to the idea of a Mongol invasion. They had heard that after the invasion of Kara Khitai plundering had been forbidden and religious persecution had been brought to an end; the Persian merchants preferred the idea of high taxes and martial law to the present exploitation and insecurity. Even the Turkish officers were losing what little faith they had left in the shah whose judgement seemed to have been clouded by his dreams and his fear of defeat. His son and heir, Jalal ad-Din, who was as courageous and talented as his father was vain and incompetent, had pointed out that none of the cities along the river were strong enough to withstand a determined assault and the army was drawn up on such an extended front that at no place was there sufficient concentration to fight a major engagement in the field without waiting for reinforcements from Samarkand or creating a gap elsewhere in the line. He had advocated an immediate attack before the Mongols could assemble in force, but his father, convinced that the horsemen of the steppes could not conduct a siege or attack a fortified position, and still trusting in his superior numbers, preferred to sit at home and wait.

Eventually news came that a Mongol army had crossed the Tien Shan mountains and was approaching the Fergana valley, where the Syr Darya turned east beyond Khojend. With fifty thousand men Jalal ad-Din rode down to meet them in the valley and when the Mongols arrived the Khwarizmians were amazed by their first sight of the invincible horsemen. Thirty thousand ragged, starving men, mounted on exhausted ponies, came cantering down the valley in close formation. As the Khwarizmians advanced the Mongols withdrew; when they finally turned in the foothills both armies met in a head-on charge. There were enormous casualties on both sides, but in the end the Mongols retired. Although the result of the battle had been inconclusive and his men were in no condition to give chase, Jalal ad-Din could claim a victory. The news was not received in Samarkand as a vindication of Muhammad's policy, but it did serve to rebuild the morale of his army and restore the faith of his officers. The Mongols had attempted to turn the Khwarizmian right flank and had been driven away.

In the Uighur country, near the source of the Irtish river, the battle of Fergana was seen in a very different light. When the last letter had been sent to Samarkand, the arrow messengers had galloped across the steppes summoning the Mongol army to assemble on the Irtish river and calling the *orloks*, marshals of the Mongol army, to a council with their khan. Among the *orloks* were men who had been with the khan since the very beginning and with whose help he had created a nation out of the scattered and warring tribes. With the boy prince Temujin, whom they had crowned as the Chingis Khan, they invaded the empires of the east, and the rise from poverty to power had created a love and respect far greater than the loyalty demanded by their simple culture. 'I was like a sleeping man when you came to me,' said Temujin, 'I was sitting in sadness and you roused me.'

The best-loved among these 'raging torrents' were two men who had risen to the command of an army before they were twenty-five years old and who had become legendary heroes among the people of the steppes: Jebe Noyan and Subedei Bahadur.

The dashing, impetuous Jebe had fought against Temujin in the first tribal wars. The story was told that while fleeing on foot Jebe had been surrounded by horsemen and had challenged them, saying that if they would give him a horse he would fight any man amongst them. When Temujin had commanded that he be given a white-nosed horse he had cut through his captors and galloped into the hills before an adversary could be chosen, but a few days later he rode unarmed into Temujin's camp and offered to serve him or die. After many years, while commanding the invasion of Kara Khitai, Jebe collected a herd of a thousand white-nosed horses and sent them as a tribute to the khan.

The shrewd, resourceful Subedei of the Reindeer People had earned his reputation by cunning. It was said of him that he had ridden alone into an enemy camp pretending to be a deserter and by persuading them that the Mongol army was far away left them unprepared for a surprise attack. He shared Temujin's grim determination and supreme ability on the battle field, and as a strategist he had no equal. 'As felt protects from the wind,' he said, 'so will I ward off thine enemies.' It was Subedei who came first to take counsel with the khan, for it was he who had been chosen to plan the invasion of Khwarizm.

Subedei's first objective had to be security. While the Mongol armies were assembling, the four hundred thousand Khwarizmians beyond the Syr Darya could advance north of Lake Balkhash and destroy them piecemeal. But Jebe, who had conquered Kara Khitai, was still stationed at Kashgar with thirty thousand men. Jochi, the eldest son of Chingis Khan, was immediately sent to join him with instructions to make a feint at the Khwarizmian right, distract their attention by engaging a major force and then withdraw to safety. They left in the early spring and crossed the Tien Shan mountains through a pass thirteen thousand feet high and five feet deep in snow. Although their supplies were lost in the snowdrifts and they became increasingly exhausted and hungry as the journey continued, they were still able to reach the Fergana valley and hold their own against superior numbers. When they came back to Kashgar their force was almost halved, but they had achieved their objective. Their feint had distracted the Khwarizmian attention, and given Chingis Khan the security to consolidate his army and advance to take the offensive.

Under Subedei's plan of invasion the two hundred thousand strong Mongol army was divided into four corps of cavalry, each accompanied by its own detachments of artillery and engineers. The first, commanded by Chingis Khan and Subedei, and the second, commanded by the khan's two sons Ogedei and Chagatai, set out from the Irtish river. The third and fourth, which had been sent south, set out from Kashgar accompanied by Jebe and Jochi. Although he had always been outnumbered, the khan had had misgivings about the size of his army and the extent of the enterprise. He had sent a messenger to the eastern King of the Tanguts asking for help, but the only answer was that if he did not have enough soldiers he did not deserve to be khan.

The first attack was launched against the frontier fortress of Otrar where the caravan had been massacred and where Inalchuk Khwadir Khan was still the governor. In the autumn of 1219, while Chingis Khan and Subedei turned north and disappeared, Ogedei and Chagatai invested the city. Knowing that they could not hope for mercy the governor and citizens were determined to fight to the last man. There were eighty thousand soldiers on the walls and it was five months before the Mongols broke through, slaughtering everyone in their path, and another two months before they took the citadel. In the hopelessness of the final massacre the desperate governor and his wife climbed onto the roof of their house and when their arrows ran out the governor showered his assailants with tiles which his wife had torn from the roof around them. Since they had been ordered to take the murderer alive, the Mongol soldiers carefully mined the building and extracted him from the ruins. Inalchuk was sent to Chingis Khan's headquarters, where molten silver was poured into his eyes and ears until he died.

Meanwhile, in the south, Jebe and Jochi divided. Jebe led twenty thousand men into Khurasan below the Amu Darya with orders to draw off any major force that might be lying in reserve and advance into Transoxiana from the south, while Jochi rode west. Jochi's task was the most formidable. His orders were to operate along the five hundred miles of the enemy front, destroying the major fortifications and keeping the rest of the cordon occupied, while Chingis Khan and Jebe worked their way round either flank. After sacking Sengar, which lay in his path, he decided to divide his army and attack the strongholds at either end of the cordon simultaneously. Sending the main part of his army south towards Khojend, he led the remainder north towards Jend.

Although Khojend fell easily before the Mongol onslaught, the invaders had at last met with a worthy adversary. Timur Malik, governor of Khojend, evacuated the survivors on to a fortified island in the Syr Darya and held out with a garrison of a mere thousand men. Each time the Mongols attacked in boats they were driven back and when they began to construct a causeway, Timur Malik countered by filling barges with archers and attacking the builders. The causeway was made from stones, which the prisoners were forced to carry twelve miles from the mountains, and defended by Mongol archers and artillery, but the archers in Timur's barges were sheltered from the Mongol arrows by huge bulwarks and protected from the incendiary bombs by roofs covered with sand. Nevertheless, in spite of the cost, the causeway crept closer and Timur was forced to abandon his island. Crowding his survivors into boats and the remaining barges, he smashed through the chain that the Mongols had stretched between the banks and escaped down the river.

Having taken Jend and installed a new governor, Jochi was marching back along the river making hit-and-run attacks on the Khwarizmian lines when he heard the absurd news that Timur Malik and his fleet were sailing down the Syr Darya towards the Aral Sea and freedom, while the Mongol pursuers trotted helplessly along either bank. Halting his army, he built a barricade of boats across the river, mounted it with archers and artillery and waited for the fugitives. Timur Malik, however, was not beaten yet. His barges were full of fresh horses and the Mongols on the river banks were strung out and tired. When he saw the barricade he ordered his fleet to turn suddenly, landed it on the west bank and cut through the Mongol horsemen before Jochi's men could come to help them. The Mongols saluted him as a hero and his exploits were recorded in the Mongol sagas as well as in the Islamic legends. It was said that Timur Malik was the only survivor of Khojend to escape. Galloping away with only three arrows in his quiver and three Mongols behind him, he turned, shot one of them down, and screaming that he had still two arrows left for the others, vanished into the red sands of Kizil Kum, from which he eventually emerged to join up with Jalal ad-Din.

Muhammad Shah was in Bukhara when he learned that Khojend had fallen and that Jebe was advancing into Transoxiana from the south. Moving to Samarkand he assembled his last fifty thousand reserves and sent them down to meet him. This time, however, Jebe's men were neither exhausted nor starving and the Khwarizmian army was annihilated.

Muhammad began to panic. He could not turn front to flank and face Jebe's advance, since his entire front, the cordon along the Syr Darya, was pinned down and crumbling under Jochi's superior mobility, while the strongholds at either end of it had fallen; and he could not commit more men without leaving his capital defenceless. His officers were advising him to evacuate Transoxiana altogether, when the news came that Chingis Khan and Subedei had appeared outside the gates of Bukhara, four hundred miles behind the Khwarizmian lines: a manoeuvre which B.H. Liddell Hart has described as one of the most dramatic surprises in the whole history of war.

It has been suggested that Chingis Khan maintained secrecy by marching round the north of the Aral Sea and crossing the Amu Darya from the west, but it is unlikely that he would have been able to pass through that part of the steppes unobserved by the Kanglis, who were Khwarizmian allies, and the overwhelming contemporary evidence is even more extraordinary. He reached Bukhara by crossing the Kizil Kum desert, which the Khwarizmians believed to be impenetrable. The Persian historian Juvaini, who lived through the invasion of Khwarizm, records that, after leaving his sons at Otrar, Chingis Khan turned north and received the submission of Zarnuk. Although they were forced to pay tribute and some of their young men were conscripted into the Mongol labour gangs, the citizens were spared, for the khan was only interested in one prisoner. A man distinguished for his knowledge of the desert was chosen from among the local Turkomans and forced to lead the Mongol army through Kizil Kum. The route that they followed, known as the Khan's Road, was used by merchants after the war.

At the beginning of March 1220 Chingis Khan and Subedei surrounded Bukhara, leaving only one gate unguarded. Although heavily garrisoned, Bukhara was so far behind the lines that it had not been fortified to withstand a long siege and the Kanglis, who formed the main part of the garrison, were more accustomed to fighting in the open than defending city walls. Alarmed by the prospect of inevitable death in the ruins of a foreign city, twenty thousand of them, pretending that they were launching a surprise attack, rode out through the unguarded gate by night and then fled to the north. The Mongols let them go. They had hoped that the unguarded gate would tempt some of the garrison to come out and fight in the open, but they had not expected them merely to attempt an escape. Next day, when the Kanglis' path was blocked by the Amu Darya, the Mongols came up behind them and cut them to pieces. While the remainder of the garrison under their governor, Gok Khan, retired into the citadel, the Persian inhabitants sent out their imams to surrender Bukhara to Chingis Khan.

With his youngest son Tolui, who had accompanied the expedition to learn the arts of war, Chingis Khan led the Mongol army into the city and rode through the doors of the Friday Mosque. At this point many historians claim that Chingis Khan mounted the pulpit and said, 'The hay is cut; give your horses fodder', which must have been a signal for the general pillage to begin, but their assumption is based on a mistranslation, and even the contemporary Moslem historians point out that, although the Mongols collected tribute, there was no disorganized plunder of Bukhara. The khan merely said that he had come to tell them that they must find provisions for his army. 'The countryside has been harvested; you must feed our horses.' When the khan had spoken, some of the scholars were sent to open the granaries, but the soldiers had already found them.

While the Mongol soldiers deployed themselves throughout the city, two of the leading imams walked through the chaotic streets to the Friday Mosque and discovered the scene that has been a source of lamentation to all the Moslem historians. Doctors and scholars were standing around the courtyard holding Mongol horses, which were devouring grain from the cases that had held the Korans, while the pages of the holy books lay scattered on the tiles beneath their hooves. Dancing girls had been summoned from the city and forced to perform on pain of death. Beneath the pulpit, singing and clapping, the officers of the Mongol high command indulged their insatiable national weakness for alcohol. 'Am I awake or asleep?' asked the Imam Hassan Zaida, famous for his piety. 'It is the wind of God's omnipotence,' said the Imam Rukn ad-Din Imamzada, most excellent of savants. 'We can not speak.'

In the days that followed the soldiers systematically drove the citizens from their houses and only allowed them to return when they had taken such gold and silver as they required. The garrison of the citadel, however, knowing that in the long run their position was hopeless, attacked the citizens and the Mongols by night and day with fatalistic courage. The citadel of Bukhara was in an unusual position: it stood outside the city, with its gate leading through the walls. Chingis Khan ordered that it should be attacked from all sides and the buildings around the gate were demolished to clear the way for an assault. Thousands of citizens were driven in front of the army to give cover to the soldiers and over them swept a constant artillery barrage. The citadel was soon taken, but, with the exception of the mosques and palaces, the buildings of Bukhara were made of wood and the defensive barrage from within the citadel had created a fire that could not be controlled in the heat of battle. By the time the soldiers and citizens were able to turn their attention to the fire they were able to save very little. Most of Bukhara had been burnt to the ground.

As he prepared to leave, Chingis Khan ordered that the walls be destroyed lest the city should be defended again, and from the pulpit of the festival *musalla* he commanded the citizens to bring forward their richest men. A hundred and ninety natives of the town and ninety visiting merchants were produced and to each of these was assigned a Mongol tax collector to assess their wealth. Juvaini writes that they were treated fairly; they were neither tortured nor humiliated and were not required to pay anything that was beyond their immediate means. The khan preached from the pulpit and told the people of the atrocities that had led to his invasion. 'It is your leaders who have committed these crimes,' he said, 'and I am the punishment of God.'

Throughout the invasion of Transoxiana each Mongol column had maintained its objective while timing its movements to provide security for the others. While Jochi had concentrated the shah's attention on his front, Jebe and Chingis Khan had been able to march round either flank. While Jebe threatened the south, Chingis Khan had marched unobserved across the north. And now, with perfect timing, Subedei's strategy reached its climax. From the four points of the compass, protected by the lines of destruction that lay behind them, the Mongol armies converged on the Khwarizmian capital of Samarkand. Marching west from Otrar, Ogedei and Chagatai wheeled left and came down from the north. From Khojend in the east came Jochi, from the south Jebe and from Bukhara in the west Chingis Khan and Subedei.

As the Mongol armies moved into the suburbs, forcing their prisoners to march with standards so that their strength would seem to be even greater than it was, Chingis Khan established his headquarters in the Blue Palace and rode out to inspect the defences. After two days he ordered the first assault and, following the usual Mongol custom, the prisoners, still disguised as soldiers, were made to march in front of the army. Fifty thousand Kanglis marched out of the city on foot to meet them; the Mongols withdrew until their horsemen were able to wheel and fall upon them from both flanks, and at a single blow the garrison was halved. Three days later thirty thousand Kanglis rode out under Tughai Khan, the shah's uncle, who had been left in command when the shah had fled on the approach of the Mongols. They offered to join the Mongol army, claiming that, since they too were nomads of the steppes, they would not fight against their brothers. Deserted by their garrison, the citizens opened their gates and surrendered. Samarkand, which had been expected to hold out for at least a year, had fallen in five days. On 12 March 1220 Chingis Khan rode through the Prayer Gate in the north-west of the city like the hero of some eighteenth-century romance. Before him rode 'the Great

Quiver Bearers' and 'the Old Elite Guard' and at his side Subedei and Tolui.

Those people of religious sects who had opposed the shah were ordered to keep to their houses and guards were placed on their doors, while the rest of the population was driven outside the city and only allowed to return when the soldiers had finished pillaging their houses. A hundred thousand prisoners were retained and of these sixty thousand were selected to work as craftsmen and labourers, while the remainder were allowed to buy their freedom for two hundred thousand *dinars*.

The rest of the garrison, twenty thousand strong, held out in the citadel for a few more days; a thousand of them managed to escape by night, but the rest were killed. Outside the city the Kanglis who had surrendered were surrounded in their camp and slaughtered. To the Mongols disloyalty was abhorrent, even in an enemy. 'A man who is once faithless,' said Chingis Khan, 'can never be trusted.'

The Mongol army camped in the plain of Nasaf and set about training their Persian and Turkish conscripts, while Ogedei studied the Khwarizmian artillery. The walls of Samarkand were pulled down and the city was only garrisoned by as many men as were required to keep order. The Mongols had been impressed by its magnificence, and Yeh-Lu Ch'u-Ts'ai, mandarin chancellor of the Mongol empire, wrote: 'Indeed Samarkand is a delicious place.'

However, Chingis Khan had failed in his attempt to capture the shah and miscalculated the effect of conquering Transoxiana. The rest of the empire was still capable of raising half a million men without the revenues of Transoxiana. Yet although the military aristocracy were now looking to Jalal ad-Din for leadership, the khan believed that the capture of the shah might lead some of the subjugate peoples to surrender. Summoning Jebe, Subedei and his son-in-law Toguchar, he gave them twenty thousand men and ordered that they should track down the shah, pausing only to destroy those cities that gave him refuge or refused to surrender.

Muhammad was in Balkh when he heard that the Mongols had taken Samarkand. Mistrusting the loyalty of the local tribesmen, he fled west, escorted only by his bodyguard, and rode through Khurasan towards Nishapur, commanding his subjects to burn their crops and flee into the cities.

Jebe, Subedei and Toguchar crossed the Amu Darya and followed him at the rate of eighty miles a day, accepting the surrender
of the cities that lay in their path. On the way Toguchar, relying on
his position, had plundered some of the villages. Such was the
discipline of the Mongol army that he was reduced to the ranks
where he remained until killed in action.

By the time the hunters arrived at Nishapur the shah had fled
north towards Kazvin, but his panic had reached such a pitch that
he was even afraid of his own soldiers. Every night he slept secretly
in a different tent and one morning discovered that his own had
been pierced with arrows. He no longer dared to hold out in any of
his cities where the hopelessness of his position had given the
Persians the courage to rise against their Turkish garrisons.

At Kazvin and again at Hamadan the shah attempted to fight a
rearguard action, but the second time he came so close to capture
that his horse was wounded by a Mongol arrow. He lost his nerve
completely, abandoned his bodyguard and eventually escaped,
exhausted, to the island of Abeskum.

On 10 January 1221 Muhammad Shah of Khwarizm died of
pleurisy. He had spent his last days in such poverty that he was
buried without a shroud, wearing only a torn shirt that had been
taken from one of his servants.

Before retiring into winter quarters on the delta of the rivers
Kura and Arax, Jebe and Subedei raided Azerbaijan. The drunken
old Atabeg of Tabriz saved his city with an enormous payment of
silver and thousands of horses which the Mongols took back to
their camp to break and train.

When he heard of the shah's death Chingis Khan summoned
Subedei to Samarkand. Covering over twelve hundred miles in
seven days, the young *orlok* rode to the khan's headquarters and
reported on conditions in the west. The khan's position was not as
secure as he had expected. The Mongol terror had not disunited
the empire and, rather than leaving it leaderless, the shah's death
had merely replaced an incompetent father with a courageous and
resourceful son. Yet Subedei believed that one concerted push
would destroy Jalal ad-Din before he had time to rally his subjects.
All the soldiers in Khwarizm that were still prepared to fight were
converging on Jalal ad-Din's banner; it would only take one victory
to conquer the empire, but, if that victory were not accomplished
soon, the empire might rally and the Mongols be cut off. The khan

accepted Subedei's assessment, but he also accepted his request not to be involved in the last campaign.

Beyond the Caspian Sea lay the western steppes that led into Europe. There were princes there who, when Khwarizm was taken, might become the new enemies of the Mongol Empire, but their lands were uncharted and their strength was unknown. Chingis Khan gave Subedei a few reinforcements and granted permission that he and Jebe might lead a reconnaissance into the western steppes, but he commanded that they should not take more than two years and that they should return across the north of the Aral Sea where Jochi would join them to assist in the conquest of the eastern Bulgars.

Subedei returned to rest with Jebe in the camp on the Caspian Sea and prepare for the expedition that was to contribute more than any other to the legend of the Mongol horsemen and to remain for ever the most outstanding cavalry achievement in the history of war.

Meanwhile Chingis Khan marched south in search of Jalal ad-Din. His lines of communication were becoming badly stretched and he had always believed that the land behind his army should not be capable of supporting an enemy, but what followed has been rivalled in atrocity only by Hitler in central Europe. The Mongol army spread out through Khurasan, burning crops, razing cities and slaughtering the entire population. When the Mongols finally caught up with Jalal ad-Din's army on the banks of the Indus, the new shah's bodyguard put up a courageous defence against overwhelming odds, but when the position became hopeless, Jalal ad-Din leapt into the river with his standard in his hand, swam across to the opposite bank and escaped. Watching from a cliff, Chingis Khan said to his soldiers, 'Fortunate should have been the father of such a son.'

On the road back to Samarkand the refugees were treated with mercy and kindness, for they were now subjects of the Mongol Empire. 'It is time to make an end of killing,' said Yeh-Lu Ch'u-Ts'ai.

Khwarizm was placed in the hands of military governors and Chingis Khan prepared to leave. 'My sons will live to desire such lands and cities as these,' he said, 'but I can not.' The Taoist master Ch'ang Ch'un had travelled two thousand miles to Samarkand to teach the khan philosophy, but the imams of Islam had thought of him as a savage and he had returned their contempt. 'Why do you make the pilgrimage to Mecca?' he asked. 'Do you not know that God is everywhere?'

Returning home along the path of his invasion Chingis Khan paused to erect a stone pillar. On it he inscribed: 'I turn to simplicity; I turn again to purity.'

2
Reconnaissance in Force

THE reconnaissance into Europe began at the end of February 1221, by which time reports of the invasion of Khwarizm had penetrated well beyond its neighbouring kingdoms. But they had not been accurate reports and even those that had reached no further than the capital of Georgia at Tiflis had represented the Mongol invaders as pillaging bandits rather than the terrifyingly effective armies of a great empire. Accordingly the Christian King of Georgia, Giorgi Lasha, George IV, 'light of the world', had not imagined that the shah's enemies would subject his kingdom to more than an occasional raid. For a long time his soldiers had enjoyed a considerable reputation in the Middle East, their armourers and sword-makers were second to none, and since the Georgian royal household had a permanent bodyguard of over thirty thousand Cuman cavalry and the knights of Georgia were already arming for the Sixth Crusade, George IV preferred to ignore the pleas for help that came from the Atabeg of Tabriz and wait until the Mongol raiding parties dared to cross his border, when their pursuit and destruction would serve as excellent training and experience for the war that was to follow in the Holy Land.

Since his accession to the throne, the vivacious young king had scorned the militant puritanism that had suffocated the reign of his mother, Tamara, and charmed the Georgian court into an enthusiastic and magnificent depravity from which it had not emerged. Yet when the half-hoped-for news arrived that twenty thousand Mongols were at last advancing up the river Kura towards Tiflis, he abandoned his luxury and, with the same enthusiasm that had seduced his Christian courtiers, rode out to meet them with over seventy thousand men behind him.

But the army that left its camp on the delta of the Kura was not a raiding party. For Jebe and Subedei the only road to their recon-

naissance of the Russian steppes lay through the kingdom of
Georgia.

On the plain of Khuman where the river Berduj joins the Kura
the two armies met. The Georgian massed cavalry charged the
slowly retreating Mongols until their horses were exhausted and
the infinitely superior Mongol fire power had opened their ranks
and left the huge army stretched out across the plain. Only then,
when their enemies were too tired to retreat at speed and too
scattered to rally effectively, did the Mongols halt and turn.
Mounting the fresh horses that had been waiting for them in the
rear and advancing under a screen of arrows, they drove a wedge
into the Georgian army. The king withdrew and only those whose
horses could stand the pace escaped with their lives. A few survivors and reinforcements made a futile stand on the road to Tiflis,
but they were swept away at the first Mongol charge and the king
retired into his capital to prepare for a siege.

In the days that followed messengers galloped across the kingdom to recruit reinforcements and scouts probed cautiously
towards the invaders; but after two weeks the scouts returned
cheering to the gates of the city. The Mongols had gone.

In spite of their defeat the Georgians believed that they had
saved their country from invasion and inflicted heavy enough losses
on the Mongols to send them back into the south where the pick-
ings were easier. But Jebe and Subedei had only withdrawn to
reassess their tactics. If they were going to have to cross Georgia
fighting pitched battles all the way, the Mongol soldiers would be
in no condition to cross the Caucasus, let alone face whatever
enemies lay on the other side. It was against the Mongol tradition
to attack a nation without first making a declaration of war and it
may be that the Mongol generals had set out for Tiflis in the hope
of obtaining a safe passage through Georgia, but it seems more
likely that the wealth of Tiflis had tempted them to stray from their
objective. Certainly an army as small as theirs would need as much
treasure as it could carry with which to buy allies in the unknown
steppes, but it had neither the time nor the strength to besiege a
fortified capital. The two generals agreed that they had made a
mistake, and they determined that in future they would maintain
their objective rigidly; they would waste only the lands and cities
that lay in their direct path, plunder only where the cost was
minimal and fight only when they were threatened.

After sacking Maragha and Hamadan to replenish their supply of horses and increase their treasure, the Mongols returned to their camp on the delta of the Kura and then, at the beginning of winter, when no mediaeval army would have been expected to launch a campaign, they returned to Georgia and raced up the east coast towards Derbend, the powerful city lying between the western shores of the Caspian Sea and the Caucasian foothills of Daghestan, where the fortress guarded not only the city and its harbour, but also the 'Gate of Gates', the pass of Bab al-Abwab that led through the mountains into the steppes.

After a false start the reconnaissance into Russia had begun in earnest, but, in spite of the surprise, George IV rode out from Tiflis with another army. Subedei withdrew before it into a pass where Jebe was waiting with five thousand men. This time the Georgians kept in close order and out of range of the Mongol arrows, but when their column turned to face Jebe's ambush, Subedei bore down on their flank and 'rolled them up' from end to end. The king and his rearguard escaped while the rest of the army was annihilated and, although they did not know it, Jebe and Subedei had defeated the last army that the Georgians were capable of putting into the field.

Riding into Derbend with the spoils of Transcaucasia and Shamakh on their pack horses, the Mongols invested the fortress where Rashid, the Shah of Shirvan, had taken refuge, but by now it was obvious that they intended to cross the Caucasus in winter and the shah offered to buy the freedom and safety of his soldiers and the city by providing them with forage and guides. As he had hoped, to Jebe and Subedei the guides were more precious than plunder, and during the armistice that followed their acceptance the shah chose men who could be trusted to lead them over the longest and most difficult route. But he also sent secret messengers through the pass to raise the alarm on the western steppes. Before they set out, however, the suspicious Subedei selected one of the guides at random and cut off his head as a warning to the others.

Although only the paths of the Mongol army had been ravaged, Georgia was left defenceless and ruined. George IV died, leaving only an infant bastard, David, and his twenty-nine-year-old sister, Rusudan, was proclaimed 'Maiden King'. She was as selfish and depraved as her brother had been, but did not share his courage and enthusiasm. She had neither the will nor the ability to rise to the crisis and reorganize her country. Writing to the pope to explain her inability to provide the soldiers that had been promised for the crusade, she claimed that the brave knighthood of Georgia had hunted 'the Tatars' from her country, killing twenty-five thousand of them, but that the effort had left them unable to take up the cross. By a cruel stroke of fate Georgia was ravaged for the next six years by a homeless army of brigands that wandered between Khwarizm and the Black Sea, led by a prince without a kingdom, Jalal ad-Din.

The Mongols' journey through the pass of Bab al-Abwab was terrible. In spite of the execution of their companion the guides remained true to their orders. All the artillery and most of the supplies were either lost or abandoned in the snow-drifts. Jebe must have been reminded of his journey across the Tien Shan mountains into the Fergana valley and the similarity did not end with the journey. When the ground beneath them became firm again and the cold wind no longer blinded them with snow, the Mongols saw that their path led down into a plain where an army of fifty thousand men was waiting.

The Cuman khan, Kotian, was already aware of the approaching army when Rashid's messengers reached him from Derbend; the Kanglis who had been slaughtered in Khwarizm were an eastern Cuman tribe and the Georgian royal guard had been Cuman cavalry, but it was not so much revenge as self-interest that led him to raise an army rather than withdraw into the steppes and let the Mongols pass. The Cumans were Turko-Mongol nomads who roamed and ruled the steppes between the Danube and the Volga, remaining pagan and uninfluenced by the settled civilizations that they had plundered ceaselessly since the time of the Roman Empire; an army from Mongolia was the only serious threat to their monopoly of plunder. Having persuaded the Bulgars, the Khazars and the Alans, whose Scythian ancestors had fought against Alexander, that only an alliance would be strong enough to resist an invasion, Kotian had put the combined army under the command of his brother Yuri and his son Daniel and sent them down to wait at the northern end of the pass.

The exhausted Mongols rode down to meet the massed charge of the allies on the edge of the plain, but with no open ground behind them in which to manoeuvre there was no hope of dividing so large an enemy. Jebe and Subedei were soon forced to return to the hills and take up a defensive position behind the rocks. Yuri and Daniel, however, were not tempted to follow. There was no reason to squander their superior numbers against the accuracy of the Mongol archers; if the Mongols did not choose to come down and meet them in the plain they could either risk the journey back through the pass and face the Shah of Shirvan at the other end or stay in the mountains and starve.

The Cumans and their allies camped on either side of the pass, sentries were posted, and they began that night to celebrate their victory. As dawn broke a Mongol ambassador rode out of the foothills into the Cuman camp. Behind him came over half the Mongols' herd of horses and pack animals laden with all their treasure, but these gifts were presented to the Cuman princes as a mere token of good faith; they were nothing compared with what the Mongols would give if the Cumans would join them and nothing compared with what they would take if they rode together. The nomad brothers of the steppes had no cause to be at war when the natural enemies of both of them were the Christians and the Moslems. Yuri and Daniel knew enough not to trust the ambassador, but although their Cuman blood could resist his appeals, it could not resist the temptation of his gold. They accepted the terms and promised to ride with the Mongols. But during the night they collected their rich bribe, broke their camp, and rode away under cover of darkness into the steppes.

The abandoned allies were no match for the Mongols. Their army was smashed, their few mountain strongholds were destroyed and the more fortunate of their survivors were impressed into Mongol service.

Well into the steppes the faithless Cumans, unaware that they were being shadowed by Mongol scouts, divided their forces. While some of them turned west with their women and children, the main body, carrying with it the treasure and horses which the Mongols could not afford to lose, rode north towards Astrakhan on the Volga. With the unrivalled speed of a Mongol army Jebe and Subedei rode after them and in the battle that followed Yuri and Daniel died, the treasure and horses were recovered and all the prisoners were executed.

On the news of the defeat the remainder of the Cumans divided again; some continued their flight westward and a few thousand more went south to seek sanctuary in the Byzantine trading stations on the Sea of Azov. Meanwhile, the Mongols were busy sacking Astrakhan.

Jebe and Subedei were no longer concerned with the destruction of the fugitives. The road to the west which they had come to reconnoitre lay open, the soldiers of the Mongol expedition were rested, richer than ever and well supplied with food and horses, and they were riding over the steppes in winter where their mastery of mobility and survival was supreme. It seemed that the worst part of their journey was over. So long as there was open land behind them and their flanks were protected, the Mongols could outrun any powerful enemy that might lie ahead of them. The two generals were at last confident enough to divide their strength. Subedei rode south-west to reconnoitre the coast of the Sea of Azov and ensure that the Cumans had not found any allies strong enough to threaten their security, and Jebe rode west to wait for him on the banks of the Don.

It was while slaughtering Cumans on the Sea of Azov and burning the towns that had given them shelter that Subedei accomplished one of the most significant achievements of the expedition. For the first time he met men from western Europe. To the merchant adventurers from Venice it was obvious that these Mongols were not mere nomad bandits like the Cumans: the soldiers wore fine silk under their lightweight armour; their discipline and their weapons were such as the Venetians had never seen; with their army rode doctors and diplomats and a corps of interpreters that included an Armenian bishop; and so efficient were the Moslem merchants in their baggage train that they were already printing cheap Bibles and selling them to the local Russian inhabitants. To Subedei, on the other hand, the Venetians had proved that they were not his enemies and it was in his interest that they should become his friends: they had no soldiers, they had not offered protection to the Cumans and their knowledge of European geography and politics would be invaluable. For several days he entertained them lavishly and the Venetians were happy to accept his hospitality and answer his endless questions about the civilizations of Europe and the positions and strengths of the kingdoms that lay at the end of the steppes. And by the time the feasting and the entertainments had ended a secret treaty had been signed between Venice and the Mongol Empire. The travelling Venetian merchants would make detailed reports of the economic strength and military movements in the countries that they visited and spread such propaganda as the Mongols required, and in return wherever the Mongols rode all the other trading stations would be destroyed and Venice would be left with a monopoly.

Subedei was now more anxious than ever to advance and reconnoitre the borders of Hungary, but before returning to meet Jebe on the Don he took the opportunity of demonstrating his sincerity to the Venetians. The straits of Kerch that separate the Sea of Azov from the Black Sea between the mainland and the Crimean peninsula were frozen. On the Crimea stood the rich Genoese trading station at Sudak which was then called Soldaia. Leading his soldiers over the ice, Subedei razed Soldaia to the ground and while he rode back through Perekop to join Jebe, the few survivors who had escaped in galleys returned to Italy with the first eye-witness reports of the merciless horsemen.

On the Don, Jebe had made a treaty with Polskinia, chief of the Brodniki, and as soon as Subedei arrived they set out towards Hungary with fresh horses and five thousand Brodniki reinforcements. As far as the river Dniester they rode unopposed through empty steppes. Kotian had withdrawn his Cuman tribes northwards and abandoned the survivors of his army to continue their flight to the end of the steppes. There they crossed the river Prut to hide in Hungary or turned south to where the Emperor of Byzantium, who was fortifying his cities, allowed them to settle in Thrace and Asia Minor.

During the autumn and early winter of 1222 the Mongol army rode up and down the banks of the Dniester maintaining their security with a rule of terror, while their scouting parties rode as far as they dared to bring back prisoners for interrogation, and the mandarins who had already made detailed maps of southern Russia collated their reports. It was the mandarin scholars of northern China who had first supported Chingis Khan in his overthrow of the decadent emperors at Peking and these men now supplied the Mongol Empire with not only its civil administration and diplomats but also doctors and scientists. They conducted a census, made surveys of the crops and the climate, drew up provisional maps of Hungary, Poland, Silesia and Bohemia, engaged interpreters to return with them to Mongolia and with huge payments of gold bought spies who were sent back to their cities to wait until called upon.

When the surveys were complete the objective of the expedition had been accomplished and the Mongol army began the long ride home, but to the north of their path the greatest threat to their safety was beginning to take shape.

After the defeat of his brother and his son, Kotian had taken the Cuman tribes north to Kiev and Chernigov to plead for an alliance against 'the Mongol invasion', but the southern Russian princes, who had suffered incessantly from Cuman raids, could only be delighted at the prospect of their destruction and it was not until the Mongols were laying waste the banks of the Dniester that they began to heed his warning: 'They have taken our land today; tomorrow it will be yours.'

Chief among the spokesmen in Kotian's cause was Mstislav the Daring, Prince of Galicia, who had preserved his lands from Cuman raids by marrying one of Kotian's daughters; although his motive may not have been entirely political, since Cuman women had a considerable reputation among southern Russians. At a council of the princes, Kotian presented them with camels, horses and Cuman slave girls, and Mstislav the Daring, true to his name, declared that he and his son-in-law, Prince Daniel of Volynia, were prepared to march down and meet the Mongols before they came within striking distance of their lands. Prince Oleg of Kursk, and the Princes of Kiev and Chernigov, both of whom were also called Mstislav, agreed to join them and the Grand Duke Yuri of Suzdal, who considered a campaign against pagan nomads beneath his dignity, promised to send an additional army under the command of his nephew, the Prince of Rostov. At last there was an army capable of defeating the invaders; the combined strength would be over eighty thousand men. So great was the Cuman rejoicing that Basti, one of their leaders, had himself baptized as a Christian in a fit of drunken enthusiasm.

Riding east, Jebe and Subedei grew more and more apprehensive as scouts rode in with reports of military movements all over southern Russia. Their enemies were converging on a prearranged rendezvous in the Dnieper on the island of Khortitsa: the army from Kursk had already crossed their path ahead of them, the Cumans were advancing over the steppes behind, the armies of Kiev and Chernigov were riding down from the north and in the south the Princes of Galicia and Volynia had sailed their soldiers down the Dniester and along the coast in a fleet of over a thousand galleys. The Mongols had just crossed the Dnieper, where they expected to meet reinforcements under the command of Jochi, when the armies of Kiev and Chernigov camped on the western bank behind them and news came that Jochi was ill and his reinforcements would be delayed.

Before they rode further down the river to join their allies at Khortitsa, the Princes of Kiev and Chernigov received ambassadors from the Mongol army. Jebe and Subedei were ready to sue for peace. The ambassadors claimed that the Mongol army had come to destroy the Cumans, who were as much the enemies of the Russians as the Mongols, and that they were now riding home in peace; if they had come to threaten the Russian states they would not now be riding in the opposite direction. But the Prince of Kiev was emboldened by this evidence of Mongol anxiety and ordered the execution of the ambassadors. Perhaps he had not heard of the fate that had befallen the governor of Khojend, or how the downfall of Khwarizm had been the consequence of a similar action, but his temerity soon changed to wary curiosity when the only result of the execution was the arrival of another ambassador accepting it as a declaration of war. This time the ambassador was allowed to return.

Chingis Khan had ordered that on their way home Jebe and Subedei should join with Jochi in the suppression of the Bulgars on the upper Volga. It was only by agreeing to this campaign that Subedei had been able to persuade the khan to allow the reconnaissance, and if he were to return without attempting it, he would be tarnishing his achievements with failure and disobedience. But, although the Mongols could outrun the Russian allies, a campaign on the Volga, however short, would give them time to catch up, and even with the addition of Jochi's reinforcements and insignificant opposition from the Bulgars, the untimely arrival of superior numbers in their rear would certainly be disastrous. With or without Jochi, the elimination of the Russian threat was an inevitable strategic necessity. To ensure that they would not be cut off and that all their enemies would be coming from the same direction, Jebe and Subedei continued their ride eastwards and, to report the Russian movements and delay their crossing of the Dnieper for as long as possible, they left behind them a rearguard of a thousand men under the command of Hamabek.

While the Russian armies assembled in crowded chaos on the

island of Khortitsa, the Mongol rearguard watched them contemptuously from the eastern bank of the river. No one among the princes had been given overall command and each retained the right to act independently if he chose. Eventually, when all but the army from Suzdal had arrived, Mstislav the Daring, exasperated by the arguments of his allies and tantalized by the sight of the Mongol rearguard, mustered his Galicians and his father-in-law's Cumans and led a vanguard of ten thousand across the river. As they landed from their galleys the casualties from Mongol arrows were enormous, but the odds of ten to one were too great for a rearguard that had been ordered to hold its ground. The Mongols were all killed and Hamabek who was found hiding in a ditch was dragged out and executed. As soon as the river bank was secure Mstislav signalled to the rest of the Galicians and Cumans to cross and set out at once after the Mongol army. One by one the other princes, encouraged by his victory and anxious that he should not enjoy the glory alone, rounded up their soldiers and followed him. Only the now cautious Prince of Kiev paused long enough to build a fortified camp on the eastern bank before bringing up the rear.

For nine days the Mongols retreated across the north of the Sea of Azov, slowing their pace so that the leaders of the Russians, who were stretched out behind them, could catch up. They were riding over land which they had already reconnoitred and on 31 May 1223 they halted on the western side of the river Kalmyus which was then known as the Kalka.

When the Russian vanguard rode into the river valley the Mongol army was drawn up in line of battle. Without waiting for the armies in his rear and without even sending dispatches to warn them, Mstislav the Daring ordered the Galicians and Cumans to charge. When they saw their vanguard charging, the Princes of Kursk and Volynia fell in behind. The charge had been too hurried to be organized; mounted Mongol archers galloped backwards and forwards in its path and the concentration of their arrows soon created a gap between the Galicians and the Cumans. The archers faded away behind the clouds of black smoke that drifted across the front of the Mongol army from the burning pitchers on its flank and when the smoke was pierced by the standards and lances of the Mongol heavy cavalry, charging silently into the gap that had been made by their archers, the Cumans broke in terror and fled from the battlefield. The armies of Kursk and Volynia divided to allow the Cumans to pass between them and before they could close again the Mongol heavy cavalry had penetrated the second gap. When the army from Chernigov arrived, not even knowing that a battle was in progress, it collided head on with the fleeing Cumans and by the time the prince had rallied his men the armies ahead had been routed and the Mongols were upon them. Surrounded and held in place by archers and hammered by the charges of heavy cavalry, the Prince of Chernigov and his soldiers died where they stood. The Prince of Kiev, bringing up the rear, halted his army at the sight of the fleeing Cumans and when he saw that there were Russians in flight behind them he ordered it to retreat. Ahead of the panic-stricken Russians rode Mstislav the Daring of Galicia and his wounded son-in-law, Daniel of Volynia, and behind them over forty thousand Russians, including six princes and seventy nobles, lay dead on the battlefield, defeated by less than eighteen thousand Mongols and their five thousand Brodniki allies.

With the roles of hunter and quarry reversed the two armies rode the hundred and fifty miles back to the Dnieper. The Prince of Kiev had covered the flight of his allies, but when he reached the river with his army still intact and the Mongols close behind he was forced to take refuge in his fortified camp: after crossing the river Mstislav and Daniel had made good their escape by burning all the galleys. The ten thousand Kievans held out magnificently against the Mongol assaults, but after three days Polskinia of the Brodniki rode into the camp to negotiate a surrender and a ransom and while the soldiers were off guard the Mongols stormed the camp and slaughtered them.

That night the Mongols held a banquet to celebrate their victory. A table, built in the shape of a box, was erected in the middle of the camp and while Jebe and Subedei dined on it, Mstislav Romanovitch of Kiev and two other princes were suffocated to death inside. For murdering the Mongol ambassadors the Prince of Kiev was bound to die, but the horrible method of his execution was not quite as cruelly callous as the Russians imagined; by Mongol tradition no man was worthy to shed the blood of a prince except in battle and all princes sentenced to death were either strangled or suffocated.

The southern Russian states now lay open. On the news of the battle of Kalka the Prince of Rostov, who was still advancing down the Dnieper, halted his army and returned to prepare for the defence of Suzdal, but Jebe and Subedei had no time for conquest. They had crossed the Dnieper in pursuit of the remnants of the armies from Galicia and Volynia, laying waste the farms, burning the villages and massacring the inhabitants, when a messenger came from Chingis Khan ordering them to return to the Volga, find Jochi and bring him home.

The delayed arrival of the reinforcements which were at last advancing towards the Volga and the absence of Jochi from a preliminary briefing with his father had not been due to illness. Jochi was an imaginative and determined commander, as his campaign in Khwarizm had shown, but his headstrong independence had made him unreliable and unpopular and when it became known that all his time had been spent hunting, his enemies among the Mongol generals, arguing that this negligence was evidence of his disaffection, began to advocate his disinheritance.

During the tribal wars when Chingis Khan had been consolidating the Mongols into one people, his wife, Princess Borte, had been kidnapped and raped by the Merkits and nine months after her return Jochi had been born. Conscious of the doubt that this cast on Jochi's legitimacy and aware of the ammunition that it gave to his critics, Chingis Khan had always made a point of demonstrating his affection for his eldest son. He had already declared him heir to all the steppes west of Mongolia, but, after the custom of the Mongols, he had chosen Ogedei from among his sons to succeed him as supreme ruler of the empire, and it may be that this had set Jochi sulking. However, the khan was a proud and devoted father to all his children and, although he was angered by Jochi's disobedience, he was not ready to allow his more ambitious courtiers an opportunity to divide his sons into factions. He hoped that under the influence of his two most distinguished generals Jochi might return to his camp where they could flaunt a family loyalty that would crush any hope of intrigue.

Jebe and Subedei met Jochi with his ten thousand reinforcements on the west of the Volga. They were no longer under orders to increase the Mongol Empire with conquest, but their journey home still gave them the scope to secure its north-western boundaries. Elated by their victories, strengthened by the reinforcements and with the added prestige of a royal prince at their head, the morale of the Mongol soldiers was unshakable.

They struck first at the upper Volga where the Kama Bulgars, rich from the export of furs and honey, rode out to meet them and into an ambush. The Bulgars were defeated, but the Mongols did not remain to consolidate their victory. They rode on south-east to the Ural mountains, leaving the shattered Bulgars to claim to the Russians that they had driven out the invaders. Routing the Saxin tribes as they went, they rode into the lands of the eastern Cuman Kanglis who had provided so many soldiers for the war in Khwarizm. Here, in the last hostile territory of their journey, the Mongols had a score to settle. Not until the Kangli khan had been killed in battle, his army annihilated and his scattered people forced to pay crippling tribute, were the Mongols ready to ride on again and join Chingis Khan at his camp on the Irtish river.

Before they reached Chingis Khan's camp, however, the journey of the victorious army was marred by tragedy. As they rode along the Imil river in Tarbagatai, Jebe Noyan died of fever, leaving Subedei alone to enjoy the glory and the admiration of the khan.

Chingis Khan had camped in a valley rich with game and while his soldiers rested and hunted, his generals, imperial governors and vassal princes came to congratulate him on his victory and report in person on the conduct of their charges. In a huge white pavilion that was capable of holding two thousand people, Chingis Khan received them seated on the golden throne that had once belonged to Muhammad II and served them the wine of Shiraz which had become his favourite during the wars of invasion in Khwarizm.

Jochi and Subedei arrived while the khan was holding court, and, entering unannounced as was the privilege of the *orloks*, Jochi walked to the foot of the throne and knelt in silence, taking his father's hand and placing it on his forehead in the Mongol gesture of submission. Without any sign of emotion Chingis Khan received the submission and continued with his audience, but the matter of Jochi's disobedience was never spoken of again. Only after his submission had been accepted did Jochi present his father with the personal gift of over a hundred thousand horses that he had exacted in tribute from the Kanglis.

The Mongol army divided to garrison the empire or to return with the khan to Mongolia and on the leisurely journey Subedei rode beside his emperor recounting in detail the achievements of his expedition. It was enough for Chingis Khan to know that his western boundaries were secure and that the network of spies and secret messengers that Subedei had left behind would keep him informed of all that went on in Russia and Europe, but for Subedei the expedition had sown in him the seeds of an ambitious dream. A corridor of steppeland ran from Mongolia into Bulgaria and Hungary where the descendants of previous invaders from the east still lived. It was land for nomads and along it lived Turko-Mongol peoples whom the khan could unite into his empire as he had united the tribes of Mongolia. Over that corridor mounted warriors could move faster than anywhere else in the world and from it they could strike north or south into either hemisphere. He had perceived the concept of political geography that Sir Halford Mackinder was to promote nearly seven hundred years later: that he who commands the heartland rules the world.

To the Mongol people, however, the expedition of Jebe and Subedei was a new source of legend and ultimate evidence of the omnipotence of a Mongol army, and it has remained, as the Persian historians recorded it, an unparalleled achievement. In two years they had ridden over five and a half thousand miles, won more than a dozen battles against superior numbers and returned overloaded with plunder. A hundred years before them the Gurkhan of Kara Khitai had led his army round the Caspian Sea and it was to be done again nearly two hundred years after them by Tamerlane, but these two powerful rulers, each at the head of his entire army, achieved little compared with the two subordinate commanders who led a reconnaissance in force while their emperor and the rest of his army were engaged in a campaign elsewhere.

In Russia the people looked upon the Mongol campaign as though it had been a plague. 'We do not know where these evil Tatars came from nor where they went,' wrote a chronicler from Novgorod, and they do not seem to have cared either. The Grand Duke of Suzdal launched a campaign against the weakened Bulgars and in the south, which had for so long been dominated by Kiev, the defeated alliance remained intact under the leadership of Mstislav the Daring of Galicia, supported by the now peaceful Cumans. But nobody bothered to reconnoitre beyond the Volga; the empire of the east remained unknown to them. The Mongol army had been so small that it could not possibly have engaged in a campaign of conquest and somehow the Russians persuaded themselves that the raiders would never return.

3
Aftermath

THE origins of the 'evil Tatars' were as much of a mystery to the rest of Europe as they had been to the Russians. At the beginning of the thirteenth century the knowledge which the peoples of Europe and Asia had of each others' continents amounted to nothing more than a miscellany of myth and superstition. As they had been told in Latin legends and by the ancient Chinese geographers' *Classic of Mountains and Seas*, each still believed that, apart from humans such as themselves, the other continent was inhabited by men with dogs' heads or even men with no heads at all. Although silk worms had already been imported into Italy and cotton had been planted in India, the Europeans generally believed that silk threads were combed from the leaves of trees, while the Chinese thought that cotton threads were combed out of the fleeces of 'water sheep'.

Trade between the two continents had continued uninterrupted since before the time of the Roman Empire, but the merchant communities did not deal directly with each other. They bought and sold through the caravaneers and market owners of the Middle East, and the spread of Islam, which had established a monopoly for the Arab and Turkish merchants, had created such a barrier that the people of mediaeval Europe had no more knowledge of the east than had the citizens of imperial Rome.

Such second-hand intelligence as did seep through the commercial gossip was always adapted to fit in with already accepted myths, which had been embellished by legends of chivalry, and endorsed, and even in some cases added to, by the Christian church. When news of the Mongol advances first arrived in Europe, therefore, it was confidently interpreted in the light of these accredited superstitions, particularly the myths which had grown out of the campaigns of Alexander the Great and the new legend of Prester John.

The cult of chivalry had led to the veneration of some of the heroes of history, whom it had endowed with all the knightly virtues, and throughout Europe a series of fictional letters had been allowed to circulate, which, it was claimed, had been written by one of the foremost of these heroes, Alexander the Great, and which purported to recount his adventures in India. Since chivalric romanticism required that some of his enemies should be exemplary as well as supernatural, the letters described a continent that contained not only tribes of fiendish barbarians, but also utopian principalities. Although mediaeval maps, which depicted India as one enormous continent made up of most of Asia and Africa, could not support the story by locating these principalities, they were more precise as to the whereabouts of at least some of the fiendish barbarians. Alexander the Great had apparently driven back the children of Gog and Magog and shut them up in the Caucasus behind the 'Iron Gate' in the pass beyond Derbend, from whence, according to Christian prophecy, they would one day emerge to destroy Christendom. It was the church, however, that was to supply further information about the utopian principalities. Although their whereabouts were unknown, it was claimed that many of them were Christian, having been converted by Saint Thomas, who had visited India to bring the word of Christ to the land of the Magi. As was often to be the case, the story did contain a grain of truth. There were many Christians in the east who followed the teachings of Nestorius, a former patriarch of Constantinople who had set out for the east in the fifth century, after being deposed by the Council of Ephesus for refusing to recognize the Virgin Mary as the 'Mother of God' and preaching that Christ was merely a man who had been endued with the Holy Spirit. The followers of Nestorius had carried his teaching across Mesopotamia and Persia to China.

It was a series of possibly unconnected events, spiced by these combinations of fact and fiction, that gave rise to the legend of Prester John. As early as 1122 an eastern prelate called John, claiming to have come from India, had visited Rome and had been received with great hospitality by Pope Calixtus II. The visit may have been nothing more than an elaborate confidence trick, but it is also possible that the prelate was a Nestorian. The legend developed when in 1145 Pope Eugenius III received a letter from the Bishop of Gabala in Syria, describing reports of a royal priest who ruled over the Nestorian Christians in the east, while at the same time a fictional letter was being borne to Rome signed by this priest-king, Prester John, declaring his intention to invade and liberate the Holy Land. Although the Christian army from the east never materialized and a papal ambassador sent by Alexander III vanished without trace, the existence of Prester John became universally accepted.

While the Mongol armies were preparing for the invasion of Khwarizm, Pope Honorius III was preaching a crusade which, although it had received some support from Hungary and Austria, was meeting with little enthusiasm throughout the rest of Europe. To increase confidence in the crusade, Jacques de Vitry, the Bishop of Acre, wrote a letter to the pope in 1217 saying that many of the Christian princes in the east were massing under the banner of Prester John to advance against the Saracens. The report was supported not only by rumours, but also by another series of those forged letters for which there seems to have been such a vogue in mediaeval Europe. Although the letters may have come from the Nestorian Christians living in Islam, who also had an interest in encouraging the crusade that would relieve them from Moslem persecution, it is more probable that their source was the same as the original report. Whatever the source, the authors of some of the letters at least realized that Prester John would by then have been over a hundred years old and so they persuaded Europe that the man who was marching to destroy Islam was his grandson, 'King David of India'.

One of the letters which reached northern Europe contained 'King David of India' miscopied as 'King David of Israel', which induced the Jewish population to make a collection of gold and send it to the invading army. Unfortunately the gold never got further than the Caucasus where it fell into the hands of Georgian bandits. If it had reached its destination, it would have ended in the coffers of Chingis Khan.

In 1221, when the conquest of Khwarizm was entering its final stage, Jacques de Vitry, amazed to discover that his propaganda had contained so much truth, reported to the pope that there really was an invading army and that it was now advancing through Persia. What he was never to realize was that there had been even

more truth to his story than that: not only were many of the
soldiers in the advancing army Nestorian Christians, but also their
commander was related to Prester John.

The Nestorian Christians who rode with Chingis Khan were
Kerait Mongols. Their chief, Wang Khan, had made a treaty of
friendship with Temujin's father, Yesukai. This had entitled
Temujin to look upon him as a guardian after his father's death,
but during the tribal wars the old man had betrayed him and it was
not until after the bloody battle of Gupta and the death of Wang
Khan that the Karaits joined the armies of Temujin. It was this
Wang Khan that Marco Polo later identified as Prester John; he
had never been to Europe, but he was the only Christian ruler of an
eastern people, and, just as the word Mongol became Mogul in
India, so, as it passed from language to language, the name Wang
came to sound like John. Although Chingis Khan could not therefore be described as Prester John's grandson, he could be described
as his ward.

A small number of Christian scholars had argued all along that
the invading army could not possibly be Christian, but most
European observers wanted to believe the story and, as more
accurate reports of the Mongol campaign began to reach the west,
they eagerly accepted any explanation that would sustain the
authenticity of 'King David'. They decided that there were
strategic reasons for the raids on Azerbaijan: 'King David' would
not be advancing into the Holy Land until he had prepared for his
invasion by securing his right flank. But it would have been more
difficult to come to terms with the march into Georgia, particularly
since Queen Rusudan had identified the invaders as 'a savage
people of Tatars', if it had not been for the fact that she also identified them as Christians. In her letter to Honorius III she wrote that
the invaders must have been of Christian origin since they carried
an oblique white cross on their banners. There may have been
Keraits in Jebe and Subedei's army, but there is no evidence that
they carried the white cross on their standards. The standard of the
Mongol army was a Greek cross made from the shoulder-blades of
sheep, from which hung nine yak tails, and it was probably a very
unspecific report of this that caused the queen's misunderstanding;
after all, the only Georgian soldiers who had seen the Mongol army
and survived had not been very close to it.

With the news of Jebe and Subedei's ride across Russia the confused opinion-makers of western Christendom at last divided into two schools of thought. The majority, supported by King Andreas ii of Hungary, in whose country some of the Cumans had taken refuge, still adhered to the theory of 'King David'. In the same year as Queen Rusudan's letter, Andreas ii reported the battle of Kalka to Honorius iii, saying that the army of 'King David' or Prester John as he was better known, which carried with it the body of Saint Thomas, had slaughtered two hundred thousand Russians and Cumans. Once again the theory was adjusted – obviously the objective had been misunderstood and King David had not sent his armies to liberate the Holy Land: he had sent them to punish the followers of the eastern orthodox church who had broken away from the true faith and the dominion of Rome.

The second school of thought, which had not been prepared to reject the theory of 'King David' and a Christian army on the basis of scholarly logic, abandoned it in favour of superstition and legend. Since the savage Tatars had entered Russia through the pass at Derbend, they argued that they were the children of Gog and Magog, who had been driven beyond the pass by Alexander, and that these soldiers of Antichrist had been released again by the devil to bring about the destruction of Christendom.

As early as June 1218 the Fifth Crusade had begun with the siege of Damietta in the Nile delta. Under an old but capable commander, John of Brienne, who was then titular King of Jerusalem, the crusaders had hoped that after the capture of Damietta the Egyptian sultan, al-Kamil, who also ruled Syria and most of Palestine, might exchange Damietta for Jerusalem. After a frustrating seventeen months of siege the sultan did offer to restore all the Kingdom of Jerusalem west of the Jordan in return for a Christian evacuation of Egypt. By then, however, the Christian command had been taken over by the impatient papal legate, Cardinal Pelagius, and, incredibly, the offer was refused. The stubborn Spanish cardinal had believed that the crusaders were strong enough to go on to capture Cairo and the rest of Egypt, but after the fall of Damietta the war went on for nearly two more fruitless years until in August 1221 the crusaders were trapped by a sudden flooding of the Nile and only the negotiating powers of John of Brienne and the clemency of the sultan saved them from annihilation by the Moslem soldiers. Damietta was returned, an eight-year truce was signed and the crusaders sailed back to Acre, where, ironically, the bishop had just sent off his second report confirming that 'King David' was advancing from the east.

Cardinal Pelagius had turned success into disaster. By the time the reports of King Andreas and Queen Rusudan arrived, the confidence of Europe had already been severely shaken by the incompetence and collapse of the Fifth Crusade. It may have been the consequent anxiety that induced so many optimists to accept the theory of 'King David' or despair that drove the pessimists to believe in the soldiers of Antichrist, but when the invaders had gone the inhabitants of western Europe were even less curious than the Russians, and their capacity for self-deception seems to have been even greater.

If the invaders had been the savage soldiers of Antichrist they would have fallen before the true cross and the knights of European chivalry; but the primitive armies of Europe had been no match for the armies of Islam, and the more advanced armies of Islam had been no match for the Mongols. If they had been the armies of 'King David', they had proved unreliable; but nobody bothered to find out why.

There were men in Venice who knew the truth, but they were bound by treaty and self-interest to keep silent.

4
Interlude

IT was several years before Subedei had an opportunity to press his case for an invasion of Europe. When he returned from Khwarizm, Chingis Khan's eyes were again turned towards the east: Mukali who had been left in charge of the eastern campaigns had died, leaving the war against the Chin to deteriorate into a series of stalemate sieges; and the Emperor of Chin had signed a treaty with the khan's impudent vassal, the king of the Tanguts.

While preparing for the invasion of Khwarizm the khan had made his will; he had known that the empires of Islam were far more splendid and powerful than his decadent enemies in the east and he had been apprehensive, but he had hoped to swell his confidence with the help of the huge army that stood under the command of the king of the Tanguts. The king of the Tanguts, however, although he paid tribute to the khan, had insolently refused his request for help and the ensuing bitterness had not been diminished by the brilliant victory. When in 1226 Chingis Khan set out to consolidate his empire in the east by bringing under its dominion the threatening empires of Chin and Sung, he began with the vengeful destruction of the Tanguts.

It was to be his last campaign. The Mongol sagas say that from the outset the khan was troubled by ill omens and although, almost inevitably, the campaign itself was a success, it was marred throughout by other misfortunes.

Soon after the march began, Chingis Khan fell from his horse while hunting. He had broken no bones, but the fall had caused a haemorrhage in his stomach and although he was able to hide his pain from his soldiers, he could not deceive those who were close to him. Both officers and surgeons pleaded that he should either postpone the campaign or else leave it to his subordinates, but it seems that, whatever the cost, he was determined to remain with the army long enough at least to supervise the destruction of the Tanguts.

Growing steadily weaker, he watched his soldiers lay waste the countryside; whenever possible they dammed the rivers and when enough water had built up behind the dams, released it to flood the beleaguered cities. Once, when the flooded banks of the Yellow River froze over, the Tangut cavalry attempted a massed charge across the ice; sliding out of control and crashing into each other they were taken in the flank and slaughtered by the unfaltering Mongols who had wrapped the unshod hooves of their horses in felt. It must have been one of the most spectacular of Chingis Khan's overwhelming victories, but he took no pleasure in it. A few weeks before he had received news from the west: Jochi was dead.

There were those who said that father and son had quarrelled again and that Jochi was plotting rebellion, but they were only those who had previously argued in favour of Jochi's disinheritance and been thwarted by the reconciliation. On hearing the news Chingis Khan retired into his tent for several days lest his soldiers should see how pain and weakness had made him unable to hide his grief. When Ogedei's son had been killed, he had simply said to him: 'Your son is dead, I forbid you to weep.'

The king of the Tanguts died in a mountain stronghold and his son sued for peace. The khan agreed that the new king and his ministers should be allowed to come and discuss terms with him, but his thirst for vengeance had not yet been quenched and he commanded his guards that when the royal party arrived they were all to be executed on the spot.

By now Chingis Khan knew that he was dying and he sent out messengers to call his sons. Chagatai had been left behind commanding the reserve armies, but when Ogedei and Tolui came, they found their father, already unable to move, wrapped in furs and shivering in the dim red firelight of his tent. Driven by delirium into despair and self-pity he had at one time cried out to his officers: 'My descendants will wear gold, they will eat the choicest meats, they will ride the finest horses, they will hold in their arms the most beautiful women and they will forget to whom they owe it all.' But most of the time the fever allowed him to remain lucid. 'A deed is not glorious until it is finished', he said and he outlined to Tolui his plans for the completion of the campaign.

Some chroniclers say that he exhorted his sons to remain loyal to each other and obedient to Ogedei, and that he repeated to them the old Mongol fable about the snake with many heads that argued among themselves for so long that it froze to death in winter, while the snake with one head and many tails found shelter and survived; they also say that he reminded them of the parable of the man who could break one arrow, but could not break a bundle. Yet he had been teaching them these lessons all their lives and as the Mongol Empire was to expand after his death, the world was to see how well they had been learned.

Towards the end of August 1227 Kilugen, the soldier and poet who had been the khan's companion since the tribal wars, was called to his commander's bedside to receive his last orders. Detailed provisions were made for the disposition and administration of the empire and even for the division of the Tangut spoils and then, after entrusting Kilugen with the care of his wife Borte, Chingis Khan died. His last words were recorded by Ssanang Setzen, the Prince of Ordos, who compiled a legendary chronicle of the Mongol Empire in the seventeenth century: 'It is clear now that we must part and I must go away. Listen to the words of the boy Kubilai, they are wise; he will one day sit on my throne and he will bring you prosperity as I have done.'

As he had commanded, Chingis Khan's death was kept secret even from his soldiers. Ambassadors were informed that he was not yet ready to receive them and staff officers and servants went in and out of his tent as though he was carrying on the daily administration of the army. Unsuspecting, the citizens of the beleaguered city of Ning-Hsia opened their gates, the king and his ministers came to meet the khan, and, in accordance with his orders, they were put to death. With the need for secrecy gone the khan's death was revealed to the army and in the storming of Ning-Hsia that followed every living creature that could be found was slaughtered.

Although instructions had been left for its completion, the campaign was suspended and as the soldiers prepared to carry their commander back to the steppes they chanted the dirge which Killugen had composed:

There was a time thou didst stoop like a falcon,
But now thou art borne in a slow-rolling wagon.
Oh my Khan.

Thy wife and thy children, thy people in council,
Hast thou forsaken them?
                                            Oh my Khan.
Circling in pride thou didst lead like an eagle,
Like an unbroken colt thou hast stumbled and fallen.
                                            Oh my Khan.
Sixty-six years thy people have prospered;
Dost thou take leave of them?
                                            Oh my Khan.

On the journey the army marched slowly and in silence, but the
news did not precede them: in accordance with tradition, even
after they had reached Mongolia, everyone who met the procession
was put to death and sent 'to serve their master in the other world'.

For three months before his funeral Chingis Khan lay in state,
while his commanders and vassal princes assembled from all over
the empire. He had chosen to be buried on the side of a mountain
that was then known as Burkhan Kaldun (God's Hill) in the range
that rises to eight thousand five hundred feet where the rivers
Onon, Tola and Kerulen have their source, three hundred miles
east of Karakorum and about ninety miles east of modern Ulan
Bator. Forty jewelled slave girls and forty fine horses were later
slaughtered and buried with him among the larches, cedars and
pine trees, and a detachment of a thousand men from the Urian
tribe was stationed at the foot of the mountain and charged with
the duty of guarding it for ever. The soil was so fertile that within a
few years the rich undergrowth had covered the khan's grave so
completely that the Urian guards could no longer find it, and
although Tolui, Mangku and Kubilai were later buried on the same
mountainside, today even the mountain has been forgotten and can
no longer be distinguished from among the others.

The reign of Chingis Khan marked a turning-point in the history
of the world. As a result of the campaigns which he began the old
empires of China and Persia were swept away, and in the west the
destruction of Khwarizm drove a small group of Turko-Mongol
refugees towards Rum and Byzantium, where by the end of the
century their leader, Osman, had founded the greatest of all the
Turkoman empires. While his campaigns continued under his sons
the isolation of Europe ended, suspicion was replaced by curiosity,
and the two hemispheres of the old world were brought together.
When the new world was discovered it was by men from the west

who had set out to find faster sea routes to the east. Chingis Khan is numbered among history's greatest conquerors and commanders, and it is perhaps only because of the horrifying slaughter and destruction that followed in the wake of his conquests that he does not stand above them all.

Like Napoleon, Chingis Khan was fortunate in the quality of his generals and many of his victories were as much due to the strategic genius of Subedei as to his own genius for organization and command in battle. The khan was a shrewd judge of his men; his highly trained officers were promoted for ability and achievement alone and were chosen for their skill and understanding of men as well as for their courage. 'There is no man alive who is braver than Yessutai', he said, 'no march can tire him and he feels neither hunger nor thirst; that is why he is unfit to command.'

The indigent nomads whom he moulded into a modern army were out of necessity expert horsemen and archers, but they were also superstitious by tradition and bandits by instinct. He knew that although they had rallied to his standard for survival, they continued to fight because they believed in his 'divine purpose' and because he made them rich. Yet such was the natural discipline upon which he built that even the seizure and disposition of plunder was organized and controlled. John of Plano Carpini, the papal ambassador who visited the Mongol court twenty years after Chingis Khan's death, wrote that the Mongols were more obedient to their lords than any other people.

Almost always outnumbered, Chingis Khan knew how to gain his objectives with the minimum amount of force. Relying on a vigilant intelligence network, he advanced his armies on a wide front, controlling them with a highly developed system of communication and using their supreme mobility to concentrate them at the decisive points.

Once the Mongol tribes had been consolidated, Chingis Khan might have been content to live off the tolls from the trade routes that he guarded and the tributes from the weaker princes that he protected. He was a self-made man whose strength came from the loyalty of his army and his own ability to command it, but the world around him was ruled by hereditary princes who presided over ancient cultures and grew rich through commerce. To them he was at first nothing more than an illiterate mercenary, but when his honest attempts at friendship were met with exploitation, deception and contempt, his awe turned to acrimony and his envy to malice. The devastation and slaughter in the empire of Muhammad II may be the most abominable event in the history of Islam, but the death toll in the east surpassed it by many millions.

Today Chingis Khan is remembered as the almost proverbial personification of ruthless cruelty, and it is true that the scope of the devastation which he wrought has not often been equalled – but nor has the scope of his conquests. Sometimes he destroyed the cities, soldiers and subjects of one prince merely to strike terror into another, sometimes so that never again could they rise against him, and sometimes simply because they had been his enemies and he had no use for them. If defeated soldiers were loyal to their leader they might rally, and if they were not, the khan could not trust them, and so he killed them. His nomads had no use for cities that had once housed their enemies, unless they were a centre of trade from which they could draw revenue or a centre of administration from which they could govern, and what they did not use they destroyed. But Chingis Khan never saw himself as the aggressor; with the exception of the reconnaissance into Europe, which Subedei persuaded him to allow, whether in defence of an ally or as the result of a threat or a broken treaty, the Mongol army always marched in answer to at least some provocation.

In every other way Chingis Khan was a surprisingly enlightened and liberal ruler. He did not use murder as a political weapon and torture was rare. The laws which he codified governed over fifty nations and were far less cruel than the laws of Islam. It is true their common sense was coloured by the traditions and superstitions of the steppes. For example, it was forbidden to cut the throat of an animal killed for food; instead it was decreed that the animal should be slit open and bled by having its heart pulled out by the hand of the hunter. It was also forbidden to urinate in running water or to wash in it during a thunderstorm, and among the comparatively few crimes punishable by death were adultery and cattle theft. Nevertheless the laws also embodied many of the basic human rights that are still being fought for today. There was no discrimination between the subject peoples of the empire, women were emancipated to make them equal with the Mongol women of the steppes and in a world where Christians and Moslems had been fighting each other for over five hundred years and where even the

Buddhists, in spite of their claim to be the only major religion never to have stooped to persecution, had been persecuting Moslems in Kara Khitai, the laws of Chingis Khan tolerated all monotheistic religions. His was the first great empire to know religious freedom and when the first western visitors reached Kara-korum they were amazed to find a city where churches, mosques and temples stood side by side.

Although he did not trust the soldiers of the defeated nations, his civil administrators were chosen from the ranks of their scholars and merchants. He rebuilt destroyed cities and reorganized ruined economies. He encouraged the commercial communities and gave them the security that they had lacked: tariffs remained constant; tax concessions were granted to speculative investors; trade routes, farms, markets and warehouses were policed and guarded by Mongol patrols; and, as a gesture to 'consumer protection', the death penalty was prescribed for merchants who allowed them-selves to go bankrupt for the third time.

It seems that the one irrational blind spot in the character of the man whom his contemporary, Juvaini, described paradoxically as 'a just and resolute butcher' was fear of treachery and faith in the power of terror. If he had not set so much store by vengeful destruction and massacre and if he had won the same confidence from defeated soldiers as he did from their merchants and religious leaders, he might have been remembered today as even greater than the other conquerors in history. Unlike Napoleon he did not abandon one army and lead another to destruction, and his career did not have the same end. Unlike Alexander his empire continued to expand after his death and did not fall apart through the petty quarrels of his generals. Unlike many conquerors he seems to have had very little ambition for personal aggrandizement.

He ruled an empire, but he disliked titles. He was immeasurably rich, but he enjoyed it only within the bounds of a simple, nomadic life-style, collecting enormous herds of horses and keeping a magnificent table at which strangers were always welcome and where he often spoke of his preoccupation with controlling his fondness for wine. He had nearly five hundred wives and concu-bines, but his first wife, Borte, who had shunned all other suitors until Temujin became powerful enough for her father to accept him, was always paramount and only her sons inherited his empire. After his death in exile Napoleon was brought home and buried in splendour in Les Invalides; the beautiful tomb of Alexander now stands in the classical museum in Istanbul; for centuries Tamerlane lay beneath a single slab of jade in the Gur Emir at Samarkand; but the orphaned prince who led one of the most wretched peoples on earth to rule over the largest empire ever conquered by a single commander lies under the trees, overlooking the steppes, on the side of a forgotten mountain.

Under Chingis Khan's will the Mongol homeland on the eastern steppes was bequeathed to his youngest son Tolui, the south-western territories, including the former empires of Muhammad II, were left to Chagatai, all the land that lay to the east was left to Ogedei, and the western steppes which had been the inheritance of Jochi were divided between two of his sons, Orda and Batu. For two years after his father's death Tolui ruled as regent until the security of the empire was beyond doubt and the commanders and tribal princes were able to assemble to elect the new supreme khan. But the election was only a formality. Chagatai was the eldest, but he was stolid and severe and his father had thought him better suited to administer the law. There were many who would have supported Tolui, whom they admired for his courage, but his father had thought him too impulsive. Ogedei was the son whom Chingis Khan had chosen as the most capable of governing an empire because he was not only shrewd and determined but also easy-going, warm-hearted and generous, and the khan believed that this combination of qualities would make him a winning diplomat. At first Ogedei feigned modesty and refused to set himself above his brothers until, after forty days, Yeh-Lu Ch'u-Ts'ai persuaded him to take the throne and receive their submission.

The warm and generous side of Ogedei's character soon made him popular with his subjects. He liked to ride along the roads with a small escort talking to travellers and giving alms to the poor; he allowed merchants to overcharge him, telling his critics that since they had come to him expecting to make a profit he did not want them to go away disappointed; and when he sat in judgement he enjoyed building a reputation for wisdom and mercy. Yet there was another side to the easy-going nomad. He had been impressed by the life that he had seen in Samarkand and he began to establish Karakorum as a worthy capital for his empire. The city was extended, public granaries and warehouses were built and a regular system of food supply was organized whereby five hundred wagonloads of food were brought into the city every day. Ogedei himself supervised the construction of an enormous, richly decorated palace: the outer walls were said to be over an arrow's flight in length, which by Mongol standards of archery could have been well over three hundred yards. He imported craftsmen from all over the empire; in the hall of his new palace he erected a gold fountain made in the shape of elephants, tigers and horses, and from the mouths of the animals wine and fermented mares' milk (known as *kumiz*) poured continually into silver basins. Around his palace all the princes of the imperial family were ordered to build palaces of their own and two days' ride away on the banks of the river Orkhon, he ordered Moslem architects to build him, as a tranquil summer palace, a pavilion even more splendid than any that could be found in Baghdad.

Yeh-Lu Ch'u-Ts'ai, who had remained chancellor, laid down rules of procedure and precedence for the new court and established schools where young Mongols would be educated to become civil administrators, having persuaded Ogedei that although the empire had been conquered on horseback it could not be ruled on horseback. He did not, however, succeed in persuading him to moderate his fondness for wine: when he showed him how it had corroded the inside of an iron bottle, the resulting restraint was only temporary, and when he suggested that he should halve the number of cups he drank each day, Ogedei childishly agreed and had new cups made that were twice the size of the old ones. As time went on responsibility for running the empire was to fall more and more into the fortunately honest and capable hands of Yeh-Lu Ch'u-Ts'ai.

Ogedei would probably have preferred to spend all his time in Karakorum, but he was bound by the will of his father and in 1231 he, Tolui and Subedei resumed the campaign against the Chin empire. A year later Tolui was dead, and as he had shared Ogedei's weakness for wine, there were those who said it was the drink that killed him. By the spring of 1234 the Chin Empire had been conquered. Ogedei returned to Karakorum, which now looked like a capital city, and in 1235, when the defensive wall around it was finished, the proud emperor summoned all the khans, governors and commanders to attend his first great council.

After the withdrawal of the Mongol armies from the Khwarizmian empire, the Mongol Empire had retained real con-

trol only over its rich heartland in Transoxiana, leaving the desolated south and the plundered west in a state of destitute anarchy.
After the fall of the Chin empire, the Sung had seized two of its
cities and presented Ogedei with an excuse for declaring war. At
the Mongol council Chagatai reported that his armies were already
advancing into western Khwarizm and even Georgia to consolidate
and expand the areas of his inheritance that had been infiltrated by
the bandit armies of Jalal ad-Din, and Ogedei announced that an
army under the command of two of his sons, Koten and Kochu,
would be sent into the Sung empire to subdue the last of the free
Chinese nations.

It seemed that the two surviving sons of Chingis Khan were
already well set on a path that would multiply their wealth and
increase their power as their father would have wished. But the
orphaned grandson Batu had no rich cities, his army was only four
thousand strong and the western steppes that had been his portion
were not even under Mongol control. The time had come for
Subedei to press his case.

With the fall of Chin the Mongol armies had already reached
Korea; when Sung fell the eastern expansion of the empire would
be confined by the ocean. Chagatai's empire was already rich
enough to finance its own expansion and that too would be limited
one day by sea and desert. Orda had inherited the rich pasture
lands of the northern steppes, but they were bounded by ice. The
poor inheritance of Batu was his in name only. Although Jebe and
Subedei had led an army across the western steppes, they had not
conquered them, and although Ogedei had sent an army of thirty
thousand men under the command of one of Batu's younger
brothers, Suntai, which had driven the surviving Saxins, Kanglis
and other Kipchaks towards the city of Bulgar, it had been turned
back by reinforcements under the Princes of Smolensk and Kiev.
These steppes were the most dangerously weak point in the
empire's defences, but if they were consolidated they would offer
its best opportunity for expansion. Subedei argued that the rule of
the nomad empire ought to be extended at least to the end of the
steppes, if not to unite the Turko-Mongol people, then above all to
protect its own flank. After that the Mongol armies could work
their way towards the ocean, conquering the nations of Europe one
by one as they had conquered the nations of China.

The last time Subedei had crossed the western steppes his

adventures had sown the seeds of a legend and his scheme to retrace his path was greeted with such universal enthusiasm that even the indolent Ogedei was inspired to declare that he would lead the expedition into Europe himself. Yeh-Lu Chu-Ts'ai soon persuaded him, however, that his place was in his new capital and that since the land to be conquered was in Batu's province, it was Batu who should lead the army.

The invasion of Europe became the principal topic of the council. Subedei estimated that the campaign would take eighteen years and would require an army large enough to protect its own flanks and lines of communication and garrison captured cities, while retaining to the end a vanguard capable of defeating its enemies in the field. All of this was beyond the resources of Batu, but Ogedei was still enthusiastic and determined to support the expedition to the full. He decreed that the rest of the empire should be responsible for providing Batu with a crack striking force of seasoned Mongol soldiers and that among its officers there should be representatives of all the families of the sons of Chingis Khan. The rest of the army, he decreed, was to be conscripted from among the Turko-Mongol tribes who still lived in Batu's province on the east of the Volga, and he gave him a corps of Mongol officers to train and lead them. The loyalty of these tribesmen was by no means certain, and capture would probably be a better description of their recruitment than conscription. But by now a large part of the necessarily increasing Mongol army was made up of conscripts from conquered territories and, with training, nomads who shared the same basic skills and life-style as the Mongols had provided some of the most reliable soldiers.

Preparations began as soon as the council broke up. Subedei planned that the army should be ready to cross the Volga into Russia at the beginning of winter 1237; by then the advance units should have subdued all the Kipchaks, Saxins and Bulgars on the east of the Volga and had time to bring back and train their prisoners. But the army which began to assemble in the spring of 1236 was formidable enough. There were several corps of Chinese and Persian engineers and already about twenty thousand conscripts. But above all there were fifty thousand of the most experienced soldiers in the Mongol army, among whose officers there were no less than ten princes: Batu's brothers Orda, Siban, Berke and Sinkur, Chagatai's son Baidar and his grandson Buri, Ogedei's sons Kuyuk and Kadan, and the sons of Tolui, Mangku and Budjek.

The army that was to invade Europe stood under the nominal command of Batu Khan, a general who had already proved himself a worthy grandson of Chingis Khan, but the real authority lay with his chief of staff, Subedei, and in him the enthusiastic soldiers knew they had an unrivalled genius.

5
The Mongol War Machine

In the thirteenth century the Mongol army was the best army in the world. Its organization and training, its tactical principles and its structure of command would not have been unfamiliar to a soldier of the twentieth century. By contrast the feudal armies of Russia and Europe were raised and run on the same lines as they had been for several hundred years and their tactics would have seemed unimaginative to the soldiers of the Roman Empire.

Surprisingly, cavalry was as much the main arm on the battle-field in Europe as it was in the east, but all its advantages had been eroded. No longer required for their mobility, the knights had become weighed down by the cumbersome armour which they had developed to protect themselves and when armies met, which without the benefit of scouts, maps or a prior invitation was not all that often, the day was decided by a head-on clash of heavy cavalry. The infantry, which was seldom more than a gang of ill-armed peasants, was used either to serve the knights in their camp or to get in the way of the enemy's horses on the battlefield.

The best defence against cavalry was a stone wall and the one area in which the European science of war did advance was in the design and construction of castles and fortified cities. As a result most of European warfare in the Middle Ages was siege warfare, where the assailants would harass the defenders with their crude siege engines and, if relief was unlikely and an assault too costly, wait until starvation forced them to surrender. Although the castles were defended by archers, their commanders, who had forgotten the advantage of mobility, had not yet learned the importance of fire-power. A new regiment of Saracen crossbowmen enlisted by the Holy Roman Emperor, Frederick II, was regarded with respectful curiosity, but the first European army to win a battle in the field entirely through superior fire-power was English,

and the longbow which Edward I brought from Wales and first
used against the Scots at Falkirk did not reveal its devastating
capability in Europe until the battle of Crecy in 1346.

Even the long experience of the crusades seems to have taught
little to the European armies. The Turks and Saracens preferred to
use their cavalry to destroy the crusaders' camps and cut off their
supplies and on the few occasions when they did engage them in
the field their comparatively imaginative tactics were met merely
with bewilderment. Since the objective of the crusades was the
capture and defence of cities, most of a crusader's experience was
limited to besieging or being besieged and that was very much the
same as it was at home.

Nevertheless, the crusades did at least offer an opportunity for
plunder and to some extent this kept the armies together. In spite
of the code of chivalry and all its pretensions, it was the crusaders
who were responsible for most of the atrocities and the Moslem
armies who adopted the romantic gestures. The raising of an army
under the feudal system, whereby barons were obliged to provide
their king with soldiers in return for their estates, worked well
enough when the soldiers were required because those estates were
threatened. But without the hope of reward armies were not easily
led abroad and after a prolonged or fruitless siege or a defeat there
was very little to stop the disillusioned soldiers from going home
again. They did not have much training, they had no experience of
fighting in unison and the personal skills which the aristocracy had
acquired in tournaments did not equip them to lead men in battle.
Under the feudal system, a man's right to command depended
upon the extent of his estates and therefore the size of his retinue;
it had nothing to do with his ability. Although various offices were
created there was no chain of command under the king, and the
great lords, jealous of each other's power and ambitious for their
own glory, considered themselves free to act independently, with
the result that catastrophes such as the Russian rout at the battle of
Kalka were frequent.

For these reasons the richer kings tended increasingly to
adopt the expensive but also more efficient system of allowing
their barons to avoid military service by paying 'shield money' with
which the king would hire mercenaries. So long as he was paid and
his side had some hope of winning, the often-despised mercenary
could be relied upon to remain with the army, and, more impor-

tàntly, he tended to know what he was doing. The courage of the European soldier was beyond question, but, as the ambassadors who were able to observe the armies in the east were later at pains to point out, this courage was no substitute for skill.

At the time of Chingis Khan's birth the nomads of the eastern steppes also lived in a feudal society. Each tribe was led by its khan, his barons were known as *noyans* and below them in the aristocratic hierarchy were the *bahadurs* who were the equivalent of European knights. The tribes were divided into patriarchal clans and, with the exception of the weaker clans who banded together for protection, each clan formed its own independent *ordu*, the Mongol word for a camp and source of the English word horde. Within the *ordu* each family lived in a *yurt*, a tent made of felt stretched over a wooden frame, and even for the rich families, life was often frugal: at the end of the winter when the preservation of the herds was of paramount importance they would travel for several days without eating in search of fresh pasture and game. For the many poor, life was always squalid. The men of the clan spent their time hunting, tending their herds and fighting: a man's survival may have depended on his ability as a horseman and an archer, but his success depended on his strength as a warrior and his cunning as a bandit. Since the easiest way to acquire more horses and cattle was to steal them and the simplest way to look after them was to have it done for you by slaves, the nomad clans were constantly raiding each other. But the objective of these raids was sometimes even more than the capture of animals and able-bodied men: the nomad warriors were polygamous and tradition forbade them to marry within their own clan.

Once Chingis Khan had united the tribes by force of arms, he began to suppress those customs that had preserved their poverty and discord. He forbade any man to own a Mongol slave, made cattle-theft and kidnapping punishable by death, and, to spread among all the Mongol people the loyalty that had previously been limited to members of the same clan, divided the clansmen among the different units of his new army. It was to be an army for which the keen-eyed mounted archers were almost perfect raw material. The life that had given them their incomparable powers of endurance had also made them sullen, fatalistic, phlegmatic and callous. They could suffer without complaint and kill without pity and they were easily led. In an age when conditions in the camps of campaigning armies were often appalling, Mongol soldiers would live as they had always lived in the *yurts* of their *ordu*. To turn these reckless warriors into disciplined soldiers required only organization and tactical training.

It was Chingis Khan's genius for organization that was to turn a confederation into a nation. It was called Mongol after his own tribe, but it contained several others that had once been more powerful: the Naimans, the Merkits, the Keraits and the Tatars, by whose name the khan's soldiers were first known in Russia and eastern Europe. It was the cohesion and persistence that he inspired and the structured military society that he left behind that were to distinguish the Mongol conquerors from the other nomad raiders. Although the Scythians, the Huns, the Cumans or Kipchaks and the Turks had from time to time erupted out of the steppes into the settled civilizations of Europe and western Asia, with the exception of the Turkish tribes who had risen to military power in Islam, they had usually run out of momentum as soon as their greed had been satisfied, and although they had defeated and destroyed, they had not remained to rule.

All men in the Mongol Empire over the age of twenty, except physicians, priests of any religion and those who washed the bodies of the dead, were liable for military service. When messengers brought the order to mobilize, trained men would collect their weapons and equipment from the officer in charge of the armoury in their *ordu*, select a small herd of horses and set out to join their unit.

The army was divided into multiples of ten. A ten thousand strong division was called a *tumen*, each *tumen* was divided into ten regiments of a thousand men called *minghans*, each *minghan* contained ten squadrons of a hundred men called *jaguns* and each *jagun* was divided into ten troops of ten men called *arbans*. The ten men in each *arban* elected their own commander and the ten commanders of the *arbans* elected the commander of the *jagun*. Beyond that the commanders of the *minghans* and *tumens* were appointed by the khan himself and given the military rank of *noyan*. An army, which was usually composed of three or more *tumens* of cavalry accompanied by several *minghans* of artillery and engineers, was commanded by an *orlok*.

All civil and military officials in the Mongol Empire carried a small tablet, known as a *paitze*, as evidence of their commission.

For the commander of a *jagun* the *paitze* was made of silver, but for the military *noyans* it was made of gold, ranging in weight from twenty ounces for the commander of a *minghan* to fifty ounces for an *orlok* or a prince. The *paitzes* of the higher ranks were stamped with symbols that were easily recognizable to an army that was mostly illiterate: a tiger's head for the commander of a *tumen*, a lion under the sun and moon for an *orlok* and a falcon for a prince.

The *ordu* of an army was laid out and run by the *yurtchis*, officers whose nearest modern equivalent would be quartermasters. They chose the camp sites and organized supplies and communications. The chief *yurtchi* was an officer of high rank who, apart from the day-to-day administration of the camp, was also responsible for reconnaissance and intelligence. By tradition the *ordu* always faced south with the right wing of the army on the west and the left wing on the east. Each *arban* was provided with two or three *yurts* to which food was distributed every day by a corps of provisioners. Throughout the camp the Chinese and Persian physicians set up their dressing stations and there was even an officer in charge of lost property.

Officers made regular inspections of the arms and equipment of the men under their command, particularly before engaging the enemy, and since replacements were readily available, the punishment for failing to be fully equipped was severe. The striking force of the Mongol army was all cavalry and for both heavy and light cavalry the basic uniform was the same, consisting of blue or brown tunics called *kalats*. Round all the borders, collars and cuffs the blue *kalats* were faced in red and the brown ones in light blue, while for officers the facings were decorated with gold and silver thread. In winter the *kalats* were lined with fur and the fur replaced the facings. Their trousers were either blue or grey, again lined with fur in winter, and they all wore thick, laced-up leather boots with no heels. The heavy cavalry wore a coat of mail with a cuirass made of oxhide or iron scales covered in leather, and the light cavalry wore either a cuirass of lacquered leather strips or else a quilted *kalat* and no armour at all. Next to his skin every soldier was required to wear a long, loose undershirt made from raw silk. An arrow might pierce his armour and penetrate his body, but it would usually fail to cut through the silk and would instead carry the silk with it into the wound. An arrow spins and turns as it enters the body and since pulling it straight out always doubled the size of the wound it was often safer to push the arrow through to the other side. But by gently lifting the twisted silk around the wound, the Mongols could draw the arrow out, turning its head along the same route as the one by which it had entered, and thus leave the hole as neat and as small as possible. In spite of the fact that the arrow head had not touched the flesh, the wound was not always as clean as the physicians might have hoped: their new prosperity had not yet taught the Mongols to wash and the soldiers often kept on their shirts until they began to rot.

In battle the heavy cavalry replaced their traditional Mongol caps with iron helmets and some of the light cavalry wore helmets made of leather. The quilted, cone-shaped cap with a thick fur brim had varied in design from tribe to tribe and these variations, together with other decorative details, were adopted by the different *tumens*. The Uighur *tumen* of light cavalry, for example, wore caps made of black velvet and yellow cloaks. From the crowns of all the caps and helmets hung two red ribbons and the fur trimmings varied according to rank. For officers, in ascending order, they were made from wolf, fox, badger and monkey skins, and for the men from dog and goat. Beneath the caps and helmets the weather-beaten faces of the more experienced soldiers were made more terrifying by the thick scars that they had slashed in their cheeks to stop their beards from growing.

Every man carried a wicker shield covered in thick leather while on his left side hung two bows, one for long range and one for short range, and on his right side at least two quivers containing a minimum of sixty arrows. A lasso hung from his saddle and a dagger was strapped to the inside of his left forearm. Apart from these, the light cavalrymen carried a small sword and two or three javelins, and the heavy cavalryman carried a scimitar, a battle-axe or a mace, and a twelve-foot lance with a horsehair pennant and a hook below the blade.

In their hide saddlebags they carried a change of clothing, a cooking pot, field rations, which were usually yoghurt, millet, dried meat and *kumiz*, a leather water bottle, a fishing line, files for sharpening arrows, a needle and thread and other tools for repairing equipment. Not only was the saddlebag waterproof, it could also be inflated to act as a crude life-jacket for fording rivers.

The bow was easily the Mongols' most important weapon. The

mediaeval English longbow had a pull of seventy-five pounds and a range of up to two hundred and fifty yards, but the smaller, reflex composite bows used by the Mongols had a pull of between a hundred and a hundred and sixty pounds and a range of over three hundred and fifty yards. The Mongol bow was made from layers of horn and sinew on a wooden frame and covered with waterproof lacquer. Unstrung it was shaped like three quarters of a circle, but when strung the outer curve of the circle bent towards its centre to form the front of the bow, making a double curve with the 'ears' at either end bending away from the archer. The layer nearest the archer was horn and the layer furthest from him was sinew. The string was more taut than on a longbow and when it was released the horn would snap back to its original shape and the stretched sinew would contract, shooting the arrow faster and with more power than a bow made of wood. The velocity was further increased by the difficult technique known as the Mongolian thumb lock: the string was drawn back by a stone ring worn on the right thumb which released it more suddenly than the fingers. In his quivers a soldier carried arrows for every purpose: long range arrows and short range arrows, three-foot armour-piercing arrows with tips that had been hardened by being plunged into salt water when they were red-hot, whistling arrows for signalling and identi-fying targets, incendiary arrows and arrows tipped with tiny grenades. He could bend and string his bow in the saddle by placing one end between his foot and the stirrup and he could shoot in any direction at full gallop, carefully timing his release to come between the paces of his horse, so that his aim would not be deflected as the hooves pounded the ground.

The wild horses of Mongolia, now known as the Przevalsky horses, are the ones that most closely resemble horses in prehistoric cave paintings, and the domestic horses which the Mongol army first rode were not unlike these. They were thickset and strong with broad foreheads and short legs and were prized throughout the east for their courage and stamina. After the fall of Khwarizm they were often cross-bred with the larger, pure blooded Arab horses of Islam, but they were never as small as has often been assumed. Recent excavations have shown that they were on average between thirteen and fourteen hands high, at least a hand higher than the average Mongolian domestic horse today, and some of them were as much as sixteen hands, which is big by any standards.

For the first two years of their lives the horses were broken and ridden hard, then they were put out to grass for three years and after that they were ridden again and some were trained for battle. Their herd instincts were fostered and developed so that large numbers could be led rather than driven – by riding a mare a man could be sure that her foal and stallion would trail behind, by riding a lead stallion he could guide a large herd – and in this way the Mongol horses were trained from birth to follow each other. Because they were broken young they were quiet and gentle. In the races that were run over long distances to test their stamina they were always ridden by young children so that the disparate weight and skill of experienced riders would not influence the result of the race. On the march each *tumen* would lead its own herd of re-mounts and each soldier would have at least three horses following behind him like dogs so that by regularly changing mount he could ride at speed for days on end, eating in the saddle or pausing briefly to slit a leg on his weakest horse and drink its blood.

Whenever possible Mongols preferred to ride mares, since their milk as well as their blood, and in the last resort their flesh, provided them with everything they needed to survive. Weak horses were often killed for food and the mounts of messengers were sometimes ridden to death, but this was out of necessity and not indifference. Mongol horses were better cared for than the horses of any other army, even in Islam, and Chingis Khan had laid down strict rules according to which it was forbidden to lead a horse with a bit in its mouth. In spite of their new wealth, the Mongol nomads still valued their horses far above all other possessions. Horses played their part in traditional ceremonies and folk lore and there was a whole period in Chinese art when all the statues and paintings were of horses, since the Mongol patrons desired nothing else. War horses were treated with the same sentimental respect as any other comrade in arms. Their harness and saddles were richly decorated with silver and the shoulders, chests and heads of the mounts of heavy cavalry were protected by armour. A horse that had been ridden in battle was never killed for food and when it became old or lame it was put out to grass, although when a soldier died his favourite horse was killed and buried with him so that their spirits would ride together. Admired for their colour, an above-average proportion of the Mongol horses were piebald and it was by colour that herds were selected and divided. Each unit of the

Imperial Guard rode horses of a different colour and white horses were considered sacred and fit only for princes.

The Imperial Guard, the *Kashik*, was the most splendid *tumen* in the Mongol army. Three *minghans*, each with different coloured uniforms as well as horses, made up the 'Day Guard', the 'Night Guard' and the 'Quiver Bearers' and the remaining seven *minghans* formed the 'Old Elite Life Guards', to which Subedei had once belonged. Every life guard was given the rank of *bahadur*, wore black armour and a black *kalat* with red facings and rode a black horse with red leather harness and saddle. Never disbanded and always accompanying the khan, the *Kashik* was much more than an elite corps – comprising all the khan's household from high officials to personal servants. But above all it was the Mongol staff college. No man could command a *minghan* or a *tumen* without having first served in its ranks and in an emergency even the most junior of its soldiers was considered fit to command any other unit in the Mongol army. A sense of cohesion and a certain amount of 'social mobility' was maintained by accepting the sons of the elected commanders of *jaguns* into the *Kashik* as of right, but, apart from them and the sons of *noyans*, the ranks were made up of the most promising potential commanders, selected by competition from among all the outstanding young men in the army. In battle the *Kashik* stood in the centre with the khan and was only used at the decisive moment. In peacetime its soldiers trained constantly, and, since they had no time for their own personal needs, were looked after by servants. They also attended councils and briefings to learn the business of command and prepare for the day when some of them would receive their commissions as *noyans*.

The precision with which the Mongol units performed their intricate manoeuvres on the battlefield was only attained after months of initial drilling and continual practice thereafter. The tradition of instructing young boys in horsemanship and archery had become an obligation under the law, but the most imaginative method of training, introduced by Chingis Khan and also pre-scribed by his laws, was the great hunt. An expansion of the Mongols' favourite sport, the great hunt was conducted like a cam-paign and designed to generate a 'team spirit' throughout the army, temper its discipline and swell its morale. For the Mongols no other sport or military exercise could have been more effective. It was held at the beginning of each winter in peacetime, lasted for

three months and involved every soldier. Huntsmen marked out a
starting line, up to eighty miles long, with flags denoting the
assembly points for each *tumen*, and hundreds of miles ahead of the
line they planted another flag to mark the finishing point. At a
signal from the khan the entire army, fully armed and dressed for
battle, would ride forward in one line, driving all the game before
it. As the weeks went by and the game began to build up, the wings
of the army would advance ahead of the centre, and when they had
passed the finishing point, would begin to ride in to meet each
other, totally encircling the game. Once the wings had met, the
circle would begin to contract with the line deepening, until, on the
last day of the drive, the Mongol army became a huge human
amphitheatre with thousands of terrified animals crowded into its
arena. Throughout the drive it was forbidden to kill, but it was
more than just a point of honour that none of the animals should
escape; if any man allowed even the smallest of them to pass
through the line, both he and his officer were severely punished.
At first it would have been hares and deer that tested the soldiers'
agility, but as the numbers of the animals grew and the predators
in their midst became as terrifying as the army, it would have been
the wild boar and the wolf packs that tried their courage. By day
the officers rode behind their men directing the drive and at night,
while half the army kept watch, the remainder slept around their
camp fires, fully clothed and ready for action. On the final day the
khan rode first into the arena to take his pick of the game and when
he had finished and returned to a hill overlooking the army, it was
the turn of the soldiers. The animals that could be eaten were
cleanly shot, but with the whole army watching there was an
opportunity for men to show off and impress their superiors with
their courage; some hunted with a sword or fought on foot and
there were those who died taking on tigers with their bare hands.
A tradition had been established that at the end of the day old men
and young princes would come to the khan to plead for the lives of
the remaining animals and when their request was granted the
great hunt was over.

Apart from achieving its obvious purpose, the great hunt, which
was controlled throughout by messengers and signals, must also
have given the Mongol soldiers practical experience of the strategic
principle that was to be such an essential basis of their supremacy,
and which Napoleon later described as the first necessity of war,

'unity of command'. To their enemies, the inexplicable co-ordination with which Mongol armies achieved their separate and common objectives was often astounding. Although their battle-field tactics were no more than the adaptation and perfection of those that had been developed by nomad archers over the past seven or eight hundred years, each carefully-designed campaign was a masterpiece of original and imaginative strategy and Mongol commanders could not have planned with as much breadth and daring as they did without absolute confidence in their communications. Through their simple signalling system, units could remain in immediate contact with each other along a wide front and through their unparalleled corps of couriers, armies hundreds of miles apart could remain under the tight control of one commander. Simple messages were signalled from unit to unit by a system of waving flags, a precursor of semaphore, and at night the flags were replaced with burning torches. As in any other army, detailed dispatches were carried by galloping couriers, but behind the lines the Mongol messengers were provided with regular staging posts along routes that led not only from camp to camp and line to line, but also deep into the heart of the empire.

As an army advanced, permanent staging posts were established along the road behind it and these became an extension of a highly-organized system of communications similar to the pony express in the nineteenth-century United States. In the days before Chingis Khan, as soon as a messenger arrived in one *ordu* with news, another rider was dispatched to carry it on to the next one and the military adaptation of this tradition had developed into the system known as the *yam*. Throughout the empire a network of *yam* stations had been established to provide food, shelter and fresh horses for imperial messengers. The stations, each one guarded by a detachment of soldiers, were set close enough for a horse to gallop from one to another without pausing and since all other travellers and caravans could rest there at night under the protection of the guards, the routes along which they lay soon became the main roads of the Mongol Empire. Marco Polo wrote later that the stations were only twenty-five miles apart and were so richly furnished that even a king would have been well lodged there. The messengers, riding at a rate of a hundred and twenty miles a day, which is faster than the record for the pony express, bound their stomachs, chests and heads with tight bandages and wore thick leather belts covered with bells. At the sound of the bells the garrison in the next station would saddle a fresh horse and have it waiting as the messenger rode in. Often the horsemen carried routine reports, gifts and simple messages that required no explanation, in which case they would be replaced by a fresh rider every day, but when they carried imperial orders and military dispatches the entire journey might have to be made by the same man. They could ride by night as well as by day, although at night their progress was slow since they had to be accompanied by men on foot with torches. On the production of their *paitze* they could demand help from anyone they met: if a messenger's horse was tired or lame a traveller might be asked to surrender his, but he was given a token with which he could either take his pick of the horses at the next station or follow the messenger and reclaim his own. In every town there was an officer whose sole duty was to govern the roads; his soldiers patrolled them and his clerks made detailed reports of all alien travellers and caravans and marked down the times when the imperial messengers rode through. In the confusion of battle, where mounted messengers might be delayed and flags obscured, orders were conveyed by waving standards and in the units delegated to carry out the orders, the officers passed them on to their men by repeating the signal with their swords.

The main body of the Mongol army advanced into battle in five single ranks, the first two of which were heavy cavalry and the last three light cavalry. Well out on their front and on either flank rode three separate detachments of light cavalry and one of these would be the first to engage the enemy. If any enemy took the initiative and attacked on a flank, the detachment of light cavalry that engaged him would automatically become the vanguard and while the main body wheeled to face him, the outriding detachment that found itself in the rear would gallop round to cover the exposed flank. Once the vanguard was engaged, the light cavalry in the main body would advance through the ranks of heavy cavalry and gallop forward to join them. The light cavalry did not usually engage the enemy at close quarters but rode across the front, showering his ranks with well-aimed arrows, or, if he was advancing, withdrew ahead of him and shot over their shoulders with equal accuracy. When they had opened his ranks and left them disorganized, they broke away on to either flank, leaving the front clear for the heavy cavalry to drive in the final blow. If the vanguard failed to create a gap, the light cavalry on one of the flanks would be sent forward to attack the enemy's flank at right angles and then, in a manoeuvre that was known as the *tulughma* or 'standard sweep', the heavy cavalry would gallop round behind them and make their charge in the rear of that flank.

But whenever possible the favourite tactic was to use the *mangudai*. This was a light cavalry corps of 'suicide troops', but their name was more of an honourable tribute to their courage than an exact description of their duty. Ahead of the army the *mangudai* would charge the enemy alone, break ranks and then flee in the hope that the enemy would give chase. The larger the *mangudai*, the more convincing the flight and sometimes, when open ground afforded an opportunity to regroup, it was made up of half the army. If the enemy did give chase, his ranks would already be spread out by the time they reached the waiting archers and when the quivers were empty and the heavy cavalry made their charge, as the Georgians and Russians had discovered at Khuman and Kalka, the result was devastating. The charge of the heavy cavalry was always the end of a Mongol battle plan. They advanced at the trot and in silence. Only at the last possible moment was the order to gallop sounded on the great *naccara*, a huge kettle drum carried by a camel, and by the time they had let out one hideous scream their lances were among the enemy.

If it was not needed on the battlefield, the Mongol artillery remained behind the army with the engineers, the reserves and the herd of remounts. When they first invaded China the Mongols knew nothing about siege warfare or artillery, but they were quick to learn and, as often happens with newcomers, they were soon making their own improvements and developing their own techniques. They used engineers for building dams as well as mining and although they recognized the limitations of the Chinese siege engines, they also saw their potential on the battlefield. The two Chinese engines which the Mongols adopted, and later modified when they compared them with the engines of Islam, were the light catapult, requiring a crew of forty prisoners to create the tension on its ropes, and able to launch a two pound missile over a hundred yards, and the heavy catapult, with a crew of a hundred that could launch a twenty-five pound missile over a hundred and fifty yards. Although its range was dangerously limited, the light catapult could be quickly assembled and dismantled and carried in pieces with the main body of the army on the backs of pack horses. The only important function of the heavy catapult was to hurl rocks at walls and gates and although the Mongols used it, as the Chinese had done, for launching incendiary bombs, they only did so when there was no other work for its crew, since, in the time it took to launch a missile, a hundred Mongol archers could shoot more than six hundred fire arrows over twice the distance and with far greater accuracy. However, after the fall of Samarkand, the more advanced mechanics of the Khwarizmian engines were applied to the lighter structures of the Chinese ones: counterpoises were fitted, making them more like the European *trébuchets* and increasing the range of both engines to over three hundred and fifty yards.

From Khwarizm the Mongols also adopted the *ballistae*. These were constructed on the same principle as the catapult with two separate arms, mounted horizontally on a frame and joined by a thick rope. They looked like giant crossbows and between the arms they shot a heavy arrow over the same range as the catapults, but they were light enough to be moved about on the battlefield and they were far more accurate.

In battle Mongol artillery, shooting containers filled with burning tar, was used for creating smoke screens, or, shooting fire bombs and grenades, for harassing the enemy lines in terrain where it was difficult for archers to manoeuvre. Sometimes the army advanced under a rolling barrage from the catapults and although fire bombs and grenades were not nearly as destructive as a sustained shower of arrows, they were psychologically more effective and created greater confusion, particularly among cavalry. If an enemy had taken up a strong defensive position, he was subjected to a *blitzkrieg*. The artillery would first pound one or more points in his line with a prolonged barrage, a technique known today as 'artillery preparation'. This would be followed by the usual assault from the mounted archers and when gaps appeared, the first wave of heavy cavalry, covered by archers, would race through and continue their advance while the remainder of the army and the artillery mopped up the enemy line.

In the last two decades of the thirteenth century Mongol catapults were shooting explosive gunpowder balls, and indeed the oldest known cannon made of bronze is Mongol and dated 1332. During the reign of Ogedei, however, the incendiary arrows and grenades were still filled with *naphtha* and quick lime and there is no evidence whatsoever that his armies used either gunpowder or cannon. But they did use rockets. These were made of bamboo wrapped in leather, could be fired several at a time from a box-like launching platform and had a range of well over a thousand yards, but their explosion, although probably terrifying, was never destructive and they were pitifully inaccurate and dangerously unreliable.

During the detailed planning that preceded every Mongol campaign, secret messengers were sent to alert spies in the target territories and bring back their first reports, and 'merchants' set out carrying propaganda, either to create panic or to persuade dissidents that the invaders were sympathetic to their cause. Maps were copied and the *yurtchis* studied surveys and chose camp sites along the intended route so that the army could live off the land. When the army set out each of the *tumens* was fully supplied with additional weapons and equipment carried on pack horses. Behind them, with the heavy artillery and the reserves, the slower-moving baggage train of Bactrian camels and wagons carried even more, together with merchants, craftsmen, and all the other trappings of a newly-rich army.

The army advanced on a front, divided into several units, each riding in formation with a centre, two wings, a vanguard and a rearguard, and each keeping in touch with the others through regular messengers. If one unit reported an enemy or if its messenger failed to appear at the appointed time, the others could converge on its position, but the appearance of an enemy was unlikely to be a surprise: there were reconnaissance patrols in front of the army and single scouts in front of the patrols.

Napoleon said that the strength of an army, like the quantity of motion in mechanics, is estimated by the mass multiplied by the velocity, and on the basis of this formula alone the Mongol army that set out to conquer Europe, moving at more than twice the speed of its enemies, was the match for an army at least twice its size. Yet the numerical odds against which the Mongols had been victorious were very often more than two to one and many of the principles developed and affirmed by theorists and strategists of later ages were already known to the Mongol 'nation in arms' simply as military common sense. At the end of the eighteenth century Clausewitz argued that the key to victory in all but a limited war was the destruction of an enemy's army on the battlefield, while his most distinguished opponent, Jomini, a general on Napoleon's staff, maintained that the key to victory was the progressive domination of the enemy's territory; with their usual thoroughness the Mongols believed and put into practice both theories. By the middle of the twentieth century military theorists had concluded their pursuit of the principles upon which the risks of war should be calculated: a successful army must be able to maintain its 'objective', the 'offensive', 'unity of command', the capacity to 'concentrate' and to 'manoeuvre', 'economy of force', 'surprise', 'security' and 'simplicity'. These were all the principles of strategy which the Mongol army had exemplified. Yet European contemporaries who chronicled the Mongol successes and recorded their methods were on the whole ignored by the parochial historians who came after them, and amateur commanders preferred to forget those defeats that had not changed a dynasty or otherwise altered the course of their country's history. The comforting amnesia with which nations recover from their catastrophes soon transformed the devastating Mongol army into just another horrible wave of nomad plunderers. By the end of the Renaissance the threatening expansion of a vigorous empire that had shaken the most backward continent in the known world out of its inertia had faded and shrunk on the pages of its history until it was no more than a bloody interlude.

It was only when the business of war had become a profession, and the professional soldier had begun to distill the principles of his craft from the experiences of history, that the campaigns of the Mongol army came to be re-examined. Their tactics and strategies were studied by Gustavus Adolphus and Napoleon and were still being taught to Russian cavalry officers at the beginning of the twentieth century. However, it was not until the advent of mechanized war that the real Mongol genius came to be appreciated and the tactical principles of the Mongol army, based on the combination of fire power and mobility, were seen to be as basic and as constant as the principles of geometry. It was in the armies of Chingis Khan that 'fire and movement' first effectively became 'fire in movement'. In 1927 B.H. Liddell Hart wrote that the tank and the aeroplane were the natural heirs and successors to the Mongol horsemen. At the same time surveys of the Mongol organization and tactics were being published in Germany, and British tank officers were being recommended to study the Mongol campaigns.

In the world war that followed, two of the leading exponents of mechanized combat, Rommel and Patton, were both students and admirers of Subedei.

Against the Mongols the European soldiers of the thirteenth century were as courageously helpless as the Polish lancers were against the German *panzers*. The Mongol army was a 'modern' army and the differences between it and the armies of the twentieth century can all be accounted for by progress in science and in technology, but not in the art of war.

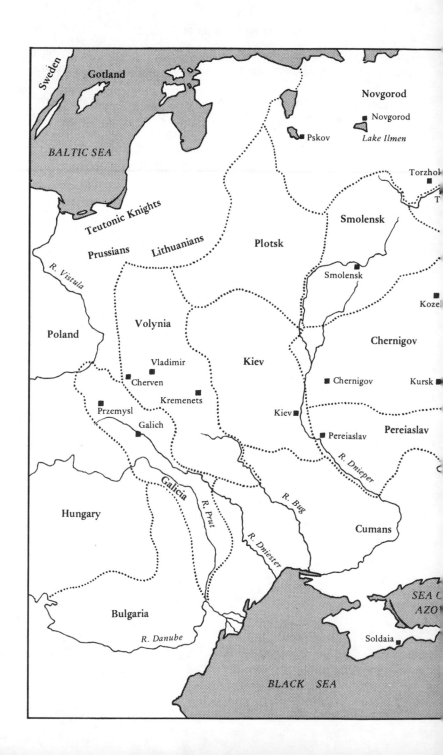

Russia
at the time of
the Mongol Invasion

Suzdalia

Yaroslav
Rostov

Gorodets

Yuriev   Suzdal
Dmitrov   Vladimir

Moscow

Murom
Kolomna

Riazan

Riazan

Pronsk

R. Volga

R. Kama

Bulgars

Bulgar

R. Ural

R. Don

Sarai

R. Volga

Kalka

Astrakhan

CASPIAN
SEA

0   100   200   300

miles

6
The Carving of the Mongol Yoke

BEFORE the invasion of Russia could begin, the Mongol army had to protect its lines of communication by dominating the steppes between the eastern banks of the Volga and the Ural mountains, and the two major threats to the maintenance of this security were the economic power of the city of Bulgar in the north and the military strength of the nomad tribes in the south. On the return from their reconnaissance, Subedei and Jebe had defeated the Bulgars in the middle Volga, but the rich capital had remained untouched, and although they had decimated the Kanglis, the other tribes of eastern Cuman Kipchaks, who had avoided the Mongol recruiting raids, were still hostile and strong enough to necessitate an extravagant rearguard. Thus, in the summer of 1236, while the 'conscripts' were being trained, Batu and Subedei led an army north towards Bulgar and Mangku and Budjek marched south towards the lower Volga.

The first surprise attacks on the Kipchaks resulted in the massacre of the outlying clans and the capture of more conscripts, but once the alarm had been given the remainder rallied to their khan, Bachman, and hid in the forests along the banks of the Volga. The Mongol army formed up in a half circle and set out to find them in the style of the great hunt. Mangku and Budjek led the wings along either side of the river and the centre of the line, which was the river itself, was made up of two hundred barges, each containing a hundred men. In one of the forest clearings they found the remains of a camp that had been broken hastily that morning. Sitting alone among the abandoned wagons was a sick old woman whose family had probably left her behind because she was too weak to ride, and from her they learned that Bachman had gone to take refuge on an island in the river where he had hidden the spoils of his bandit raids. When the Mongols' wing reached the river bank opposite the island, their barges were far behind and there was such a strong wind blowing in from the steppes that the river was too rough for armed men and horses to swim in it; but the spreading currents blown by the wind revealed a sandbank beneath the water where it was shallow enough for the army to ford. Not realizing that the Mongols would be able to cross, Bachman was taken by surprise and within an hour all his men had been either slaughtered on the island or drowned in the river, the booty had been taken and he and Prince Catchar of the Alans were prisoners with the women and children. When he was led before Mangku, Bachman refused to kneel. 'Do you think I am a camel?' he said, and rather than plead for mercy he asked for the honour to die by Mangku's own hand. Mangku, however, preferred to assign that privilege to his brother, and Bachman and Catchar were both cut in half by Budjek's sword.

In the north Batu and Subedei were greeted by the oppressed Slav peasants as though they were liberators since wealth had made the Bulgar hunters and merchants haughty and tyrannical. The lands between the Kama and the Volga had once been the home of all the Bulgars, but in the middle of the seventh century many of them had migrated to the Danube and founded the nation that bears their name today. It was the descendants of those who had remained who had abandoned their nomadic life, become the most northern converts to Islam, grown rich in the fur trade, imported Slavs and Finns to work for them and built themselves the beautiful city of Bulgar. Before the spring of 1237 the Bulgar kingdom of the middle Volga had become a vassal state of the Mongol Empire and the fate of its capital remains unrecorded. All that is known is that the population of over fifty thousand was exterminated and the city so utterly destroyed that it was never rebuilt.

Before they returned to join the rest of the army, Batu and Subedei swept the foothills of the Urals, receiving the submission of the Bashkirs and bringing back more conscripts for their auxiliaries. At the beginning of winter 1237, just as Subedei had planned, a Mongol army of a hundred and twenty thousand men crossed the frozen Volga into Russia.

There was still no unity among the Russian states, whose con-t tentious rulers had seen the campaign against the Bulgars as just another raid, and Subedei hoped that by the time they realized that the Mongol objective was conquest, his advance would have struck deep enough to divide them physically, his policy of deliberate and total destruction would have panicked their subjects and his route would have kept them guessing, so forcing each prince to remain at home lest his land should be the first to face invasion. He knew that the most powerful prince was the Grand Duke Yuri of Suzdal, whose army had turned back after its allies had been defeated at Kalka, and Subedei's plan was to drive his corridor of terror through the centre of Russia, dividing the lands of Suzdal and Novgorod from the lands of Chernigov and Kiev, and then turn back to outflank isolated Suzdal.

Riding through the thick forest on the west bank of the Volga the Mongol army entered Russia unobserved. The weak point on the Russian boundary was Riazan, a small vassal state of Suzdal which lay between Suzdal and Chernigov and which was governed by a family of princes whose rivalry was excessive even by Russian standards. Each prince had his own province and city: two brothers, Yuri and Roman, ruled from Riazan and Isteslawetz and their cousins Oleg and Yaroslav from Pronsk and Murom. When the Mongols appeared suddenly in their lands, Yuri, Oleg and Yaroslav assembled their armies at Riazan, and Roman, protected by his own army, rode north to the city of Vladimir in Suzdalia, to appeal for help from their overlord. But the grand duke simply answered that if they ceased quarrelling and united their armies they would easily be able to contain the Mongols on their own.

Meanwhile at Riazan the other princes had received a Mongol ambassador demanding the surrender of their principality and a tax of one tenth of all their wealth and supplies for the Mongol army. Shouting from the walls of their city they had replied that when they were gone the Mongols could have everything. The ambassador was a woman, accompanied by only two Mongol officers, and probably chosen as an interpreter from a nomad tribe. Such was the superstition of the Russians, however, that she was not even allowed through the gates of the city, and the chroniclers say that she was a sorceress.

Subedei and Batu had expected the demand to be refused and the Mongol army was ready and waiting when the three princes rode out to meet it. The Mongol victory, however, was not decisive. The princes broke up at the first charge and withdrew to take refuge behind the walls of their cities.

It was time for the terror to begin. The Mongol army advanced on Riazan, laying waste the land and sacking all the towns and cities, including Isteslawetz and Pronsk. When the Mongols laid siege to a city in forested country, their engineers surrounded it with a wooden palisade which not only prevented its messengers from escaping, but also gave cover to the archers and artillery and offered a defence and a barrier against a relieving army. At Riazan the stockade was completed in only nine days, and after a bombardment of five days, the city was stormed and taken, three days before Christmas. The artillery had only launched rocks, so the fire-raising that followed the city's capture must have seemed all the more brutally callous and savage. Prince Yuri, his family and all their courtiers were slaughtered. Some of his people were shot in the streets or flayed alive, others were impaled and left to die in the burning buildings. Even the churches were set on fire, and before they all died, the monks and the citizens who had taken refuge with them watched helplessly as all the young women, including the nuns, were systematically raped. Only at the end were a few survivors allowed to escape so that the news of the terror might spread.

When the Mongols moved on to Kolomna, the last city of Riazan, the Grand Duke of Suzdal began to take notice, his own nearest town, Moscow, being only fifty miles further on. Roman, who no longer had a capital of his own, was marching west to defend Kolomna, and the grand duke sent his own army to join him under his son Prince Vsevolod and his commander-in-chief, Ermei Glebovich. He also sent a detachment under his son Prince Vladimir to reinforce Moscow, which, although it was not yet a great city, was big enough to have a substantial garrison. Meanwhile, messengers were dispatched to the rest of his powerful family, asking them to assemble their armies in the north on the banks of the river Siti, and above all to his brother, Prince Yaroslav of Novgorod, beseeching him to join them.

The relieving army never reached Kolomna. Prince Vsevolod returned to Vladimir with the news that it had been intercepted and forced to take up a defensive position on a hill outside the city. Just before the Mongols had completely surrounded it, he and a small detachment had escaped, leaving Prince Roman and General Glebovich to die with the rest of their soldiers.

When Kolomna had been taken and suffered the same fate as Riazan, the Mongol army entered Suzdalia and stormed Moscow.

In the general slaughter the military governor was killed, but this time they were ready to take prisoners to swell the labour gangs for their engineers, and among the prisoners was Prince Vladimir.

On receipt of the news that the Mongols were attacking Moscow, the grand duke set out at once to rendezvous with his brothers and nephews, leaving his wife and his two sons Vsevolod and Mstislav in Vladimir, which he believed was strong enough to hold out until he returned with an army. But from Moscow the Mongol army turned back and rode the hundred miles to Vladimir without stopping. Outside its 'Golden Gate' they asked if the grand duke was still in the city and when the garrison's only answer was a shower of arrows, they held up their wretched prisoner, Prince Vladimir, and demanded a surrender in return for his life. The grand duke's other two sons could do nothing but refuse and their brother was executed in front of them. Mongol officers then rode ostentatiously round the walls of the city inspecting its defences. The engineers had brought the logs for their palisades with them from Riazan and when they had invested the city, Subedei dispatched a vanguard to find the grand duke and watch him, and sent half the army twenty-five miles north to storm the city of Suzdal.

The 'Mongol terror' seems all the more abominable because it had been so calculated, but now that it had achieved its purpose and reduced the civil population of Suzdalia to hopeless confusion, the indiscriminate slaughter began to be reduced, if for no other reason, than because it was a waste of time and because there was always a use for able-bodied prisoners. Suzdal was taken at the first assault, but the priests and nuns were spared, and within five days the assailants had returned to their camp outside Vladimir with thousands of prisoners.

On Saturday, 7 February 1238, the assault on Vladimir began. All day and all night the artillery bombarded the city with rocks, while the soldiers built scaffolding and brought up battering rams, and at dawn on Sunday they stormed all four gates at once. In spite of its large garrison, the panic of the citizens had created such chaos that Vladimir was impossible to defend. By midday the Mongols had reached the old centre of the city and the Princes Vsevolod and Mstislav were dead. The bishop took the grand duchess, her daughters and grandchildren into the cathedral where hundreds were already sheltering, barricaded the door and hid them in the choir loft, but the Mongol soldiers had seen them. When the refugees in the main body of the church tried to put up a defence, they broke down the door and slaughtered them. They may have wanted to take the royal family as hostages, but the grand duchess refused to be tempted down from the choir loft, so the soldiers brought in straw and faggots and set fire to the building. The royal family were burned to death, and as the cathedral crumbled their scorched bodies fell among the other corpses in the nave, where lay also the torn remains of the precious icon of the Madonna that had in the past wrought so many miracles for the people of Vladimir.

After the fall of Vladimir, Subedei decided that it was time to divide: he would ride due north to destroy the grand duke's army, while Batu would ride north-east, forcing Novgorod to remain on the defensive and eventually investing the capital where Subedei would join him. As they marched, both armies sacked the cities that lay in their path: Batu took Dmitrov and Tver and Subedei took Yuriev, Rostov and Yaroslav.

While Subedei marched north the grand duke did nothing. At first it might have been wise to assemble his last army out of reach of the enemy and in a position from which it could march down to meet them, whatever road they took, but every day he was becoming more isolated and the Mongol army was the one invader that was not going to be absorbed by the vastness of the Russian countryside or worn down by the harshness of its winter. He already had an army on the banks of the Siti – his brother Sviatoslav and his nephews Vsevolod, Vladimir and Vasilko, the Prince of Rostov, had joined him – but their faith was in the force of numbers, so they went on waiting anxiously for the army from Novgorod that was not even on its way. At the end of February the grand duke sent out a reconnaissance of three thousand men to discover the whereabouts of the invaders. After only a few days their commander brought them back with a simple report that has been recorded by the chroniclers: 'My lord, the Tatars have surrounded us.'

On 4 March the Mongol army appeared and the last hopes of Suzdalian resistance were crushed. The Russian army was scattered, the grand duke was killed in the battle and Prince Vasilko of Rostov was taken prisoner, never to be seen again.

In the lands of Novgorod, within striking distance of its capital, the first city which Batu reached and destroyed was Torzhok. But it was courageously defended and its capture cost him two vital weeks. When he set out again the early spring thaw had begun, the ice and snow melted, the rivers that run into lake Ilmen flooded their banks and the southern Novgorodian farm lands became a maze of marshes. In the heart of enemy country the Mongol army had lost the advantage of mobility, and sixty miles short of the city of Novgorod, Batu Khan turned back.

United again, Subedei and Batu rode south to spend the summer in the empty steppes on the west of the Don. For some time Chernigov had been garrisoning its cities and preparing its defences to face an invasion, but the Mongols were short of supplies and they chose to ride across its north, avoiding the cities, rather than retrace their steps through the countryside that they had devastated. The garrison of Kozelsk, however, fearing the fate of its neighbours, left its gates and rode out to intercept them; wheeling to cover their attack the Mongol vanguard was overwhelmed. The defeat was humiliating and costly, although the casualties were probably not as many as the four thousand that the Russian chroniclers claim, and the Mongols halted to avenge it. For seven desperate weeks, longer than any other Russian city, Kozelsk held out, but in the end it fell and its population was exterminated in such a hideous slaughter that the Mongols themselves renamed it the 'City of Sorrow'.

In the green steppeland of the Don basin, in country now known as the western Ukraine, the Mongol army camped and rested for the summer. Fresh herds of horses were brought in from Mongolia and during the following winter the herds and supplies were further augmented by a series of raids and the systematic destruction of the other nomad nations: Siban, Budjek and Buri sacked Murom and Gorodets and rode 'so far north that there was hardly any night'. Mangku defeated the Circassians and the Alans and plundered the northern Caucasus, and Berke rode west to raid the refugees from Bachman's tribes and the Cuman clans with whom they had settled.

So vast were the numbers of Cuman, Circassian and Alan prisoners that they almost outnumbered their Mongol captors. Most of them were sold into slavery, and many thousands were bought by the new Sultan of Egypt, al-Salih' to augment his Turkoman army. Yet ignominious slavery was not to be the end of their struggle with the Mongols. Several times in the past the Turkoman mercenaries and slave-soldiers that had served in the armies of the Moslem princes had risen to establish an oligarchy of their own. The new slaves became part of the most powerful cavalry unit in the Egyptian army, and within twelve years of their capture, one of their leaders, Aybak, had married Queen Shajar al-Durr, founded the Burji dynasty and become the first Mamluk sultan of Egypt – in 1260 they were to meet the Mongols again, on the battlefield of Ain Jalut.

In spite of Berke's raids, most of the Cumans had escaped into the west towards the border of Galicia. Their khan, Kotian, had learned from past experience that it was useless to stand and fight against the Mongols, but it was clear to him that when the invasion campaign began again, he would not be able to avoid them without leaving Russia altogether, and the obvious place to seek refuge was Hungary. After Subedei's first campaign in southern Russia, some Cuman refugees had been allowed to settle in Hungary, and as a result of an expansionist policy by which the Hungarians hoped to extend their rule over the nomads as far as the Bashkirs in the foothills of the Urals (which were then known as Greater Hungary) the Hungarians had begun to send missionaries to convert the nomads to Christianity. After his accession to the throne of Hungary in 1235, King Bela IV had gone so far as to take the title of king of the Cumans and the most prominent of his missionaries was a Dominican friar, called Julian, whom Kotian had met. During the invasion of Riazan and Suzdal, Friar Julian had forsaken his mission to observe and report the campaign, and he had even interviewed two Mongol officers who had been intercepted by one of the Suzdalian patrols, while on their way to deliver a letter to his master, King Bela. Although his report contained the usual hearsay about the Mongols' wealth and their golden palaces, it also gave an ominously accurate assessment of their military prowess and their matchless mobility. The letter which had been intercepted demanded a surrender and compensation from King Bela for sheltering their Cuman enemies, and claimed that the last three emissaries sent to the court of Hungary had never returned. This demand, which, if nothing else, served as a warning, should have arrived before the news of the Mongol atrocities and it may be that Batu, whose intelligence reports had made him well aware of the Hungarian ambitions in the southern steppes, had written so early to King Bela in the hope of tempting him into an ill-prepared, pre-emptive campaign. But whatever its intent, the letter's threats, combined with Friar Julian's reports, left Bela in no doubt that if Chernigov and Kiev fell Hungary would be next. Although the Hungarian army was potentially the strongest in Europe, it was no surprise to Kotian that when he asked for asylum in return for the loyalty of his forty thousand warriors and a promise that the Cumans would be converted to Christianity, King Bela granted the request with such anxious enthusiasm that he even volunteered to be godfather at Kotian's christening.

It was when the Mongol army had reassembled at its camp and all the princes were together again that the first symptoms of family discord and jealousy began to emerge. Batu had begun by being self-conscious and awed by his position in so powerful an army. The early death of his father, whose legitimacy he knew had been doubted, had left him the youngest and the poorest of Chingis Khan's heirs and made him rank above the other princes of his own generation. Yet, although he was now carving an empire of his own, the army that conquered in his name was not his, and he was aware that it contained both envious princes who would one day be more powerful than he was, and experienced officers who rightly attributed their enormous success to the genius of his chief of staff. All this had made him anxious to prove himself, but also cautious lest he should be seen to fail, and the trivial defensive criticisms and over-sensitive self-importance that this insecurity induced were a constant irritation to his otherwise elated staff corps.

As often happens, it was a petty squabble that brought the ill-feeling to the surface. The Mongol custom was that at a feast the senior prince present should drink first, and at a banquet held to celebrate the imminent renewal of the Russian invasion, Batu, perhaps inadvertently, drank before the other princes. He was, after all, the khan and, as he later pointed out, also the oldest. But his apparent assumption of superiority, which may have offended all the members of the imperial family who considered themselves to be equals, so infuriated Kuyuk and Buri that they stormed out of the banqueting tent hurling insults at him. It was no more than an embarrassing display of temper, but, to the exasperation of the other princes, Batu aggravated the discord by writing to Ogedei describing the incident and complaining that the two princes had insulted him in public and left the feast without his consent. The first Mongol book, *The Secret History of the Mongols*, compiled at an unknown date from stories and legends about Chingis Khan and the early years of Ogedei's reign, contains a record of Batu's letter and if the record is at all accurate there would seem to be some justification for Buri's description of him as an old woman. The letter was awkward enough for Buri, whose grandfather, Chagatai, was the rigid minister of the law at Karakorum, but for Ogedei's son Kuyuk it was alarming. He knew that there was already a strong faction at the Mongol court, led by his mother's family, that was lobbying for his nomination as successor to his father as supreme khan, and if Batu's charges went unanswered his chances might be ruined.

Kuyuk went back to Karakorum, but by the time he arrived his father had already been so incensed by the letter that he was threatening to have him placed in the front ranks of the army and to recall Buri for punishment by his grandfather. So great was his anger that he refused even to see his son, and he was only dissuaded from passing sentence on the insubordinate princes by Chagatai's notoriously stubborn and unequivocal adherence to the rules of legal procedure. In his code of laws Chingis Khan had ruled that on active service all disputes were to be settled by the commander in the field, and Chagatai insisted that only Batu had jurisdiction to punish the princes. Ogedei relented, but before Kuyuk rejoined the army he was granted an audience at which he was left in no doubt that an expendable commander such as himself was in no position to jeopardize the campaign with displays of temperament.

Meanwhile someone had reasoned with Batu. Both Kuyuk and Buri returned to their commands and there is no record of their having suffered any punishment, but beneath the surface there remained a festering family animosity that would one day play its part in the disintegration of the Mongol Empire.

It was not until the summer of 1240 that the invasion of Russia began again. The Mongol army spread out and the lands of Pereiaslav and Chernigov suffered the same fate as Riazan and Suzdalia. The countryside was wasted, the city of Pereiaslav was left in ashes and after a desperate resistance in which the defenders were reduced to dislodging the stones from their own battlements and pushing them onto the enemy, the city of Chernigov was taken and destroyed. By the middle of November the vanguard under the command of Mangku had reached Kiev and Prince

Daniel, who had succeeded Mstislav in Galicia, his brother Prince Vasilko of Volynia and Prince Michael of Chernigov, had all fled to find refuge in Hungary or Poland.

To the Russians, Kiev was 'the mother of cities'. Standing on the high banks above the marshes of the river Dnieper, along which for four hundred years the ships that traded with Byzantium had brought its wealth and its culture, the golden domes of thirty churches gleamed above its white walls. Even to the invaders who had seen the splendour of Samarkand it was beautiful, and they called it 'the court of the golden heads'. The governor, Dimitri, who had been appointed by Prince Daniel of Galicia, was determined to defend Kiev at all costs, but there were many who believed that they might save their beloved city by surrendering and paying whatever tribute the Mongols demanded, and so, when Mangku's ambassadors came to call for its surrender, Dimitri killed them and sealed its fate.

When Batu arrived, the storming of the city began. Although it was surrounded, the artillery concentrated its bombardment on the Polish Gate where even the battlements were made of wood and when the gate fell the heavy cavalry clattered into the streets that had been showered all day by Mongol arrows. Exhausted by their attack, the Mongols spent the first night on the city walls, and the next day, 6 December 1240, Kiev was taken street by street. The final stronghold was the Church of the Virgin, that had been hurriedly fortified during the night, but when the Mongols attacked, so many terrified citizens climbed onto the roof and into the tower that the building collapsed, not only killing the refugees who had caused it to fall, but also crushing the defenders inside and suffocating the people who were trying to tunnel their way out. Dimitri, who had been severely wounded in the fighting, was brought before Batu, but his courage and his loyalty to a prince who had abandoned him had earned him the respect of his captors and he was allowed to go free.

The city that had once ruled Russia was utterly destroyed and plundered. All the Byzantine treasures were carried away and even the tombs of the saints were broken open and their bones scattered. Among the irreplaceable ruins, the only building that remained intact was the magnificent cathedral of Saint Sophia, containing the tomb of its builder, Yaroslav the Wise, the man who had revised and codified the Russian laws and established Kiev as the political and religious capital of Russia – an apposite example of the Mongol sense of values.

After the fall of Kiev the Mongol armies advanced against no more than token resistance. Within three weeks they had reached the western border of Russia and the Carpathian mountains that formed a natural bulwark around Hungary. Volynia and Galicia were overrun; Kremenets, the Volynian city of Vladimir, Cherven, Przemysl and Galich were captured and plundered; many smaller towns and cities were wiped off the map for ever; and the lesser princes who had not fled with their masters surrendered their estates to Batu.

When the campaign was over, the Mongol commanders assembled at Batu's camp near Przemysl, and Subedei outlined his audacious plan for the invasion of Europe. Although the strength of the army had been greatly increased by the conquest of the nomads in the Russian steppes and only thirty thousand men were to be left behind to maintain control in Russia, the combined strength of the *tumens* available for the invasion can not have been more than a hundred thousand men; yet the further campaign was to be the crowning achievement of Subedei's genius, eclipsing even the masterly conquest of Transoxiana. Hungary was the first objective, but its subjugation could not be achieved without neutralizing the offensive capacity of its neighbours and, on a dimension that was awesome for its age, Subedei planned that the Mongol armies would advance between the Baltic and the Black Sea on a front of over six hundred miles. Of all the imperial princes, Baidar, son of Chagatai, and Kadan, son of Ogedei, must have been the two who had earned the most confidence and respect from the great general, since it was to them that he assigned a formidable task. With only two *tumens* (twenty thousand men) they were to sweep north of the Carpathians into Poland and Lithuania, distracting, containing and if possible crushing all threats to the security of the invasion. Once the invasion was established, they were to strike down from the north to support the rest of the army which would have entered Hungary through the mountain passes in a three-pronged attack. In the centre the main body under Batu and the other princes would strike directly across the Carpathians with one *tumen* on its northern flank under the command of Siban, Batu's brother, and in the south three *tumens* under Subedei and Kuyuk. Once the main Hungarian army had been located, the invaders, as always remaining in contact through signals and messengers, would unite in sufficient strength to destroy it and withdraw ahead of it, luring it into the field, until Baidar and Kadan could report that any threat from Poland had been neutralized. The commanders returned to their units and at the beginning of 1241 the campaign began.

Southern and eastern Russia were left in ruins. For the time being Novgorod had escaped, but it was beset by other enemies and although the Mongols had left so few soldiers behind, it was in no position to challenge them. While the Mongol armies had been advancing through Chernigov, the Knights of the Brotherhood of the Sword from Livonia on the Baltic coast, who had joined the Teutonic Order, had attempted to take Pskov in the east, and an army of Swedes under Earl Birger had landed in the mouth of the river Neva in the north. After so much panic in the face of the Mongols, the victories over these lesser invaders were a joyous consolation to the people of Novgorod. The Livonian Knights were forced to retreat, and at the Neva the Swedes were so decisively defeated by Yaroslav of Novgorod's young son Prince Alexander that he was given the title Alexander Nevsky.

For the rest of Russia the worst of the fighting was over, but what Karl Marx described as 'the bloody swamp of Mongol slavery' was only just beginning. The next two hundred years of Russian history were to be known as the period of 'the Mongol yoke'.

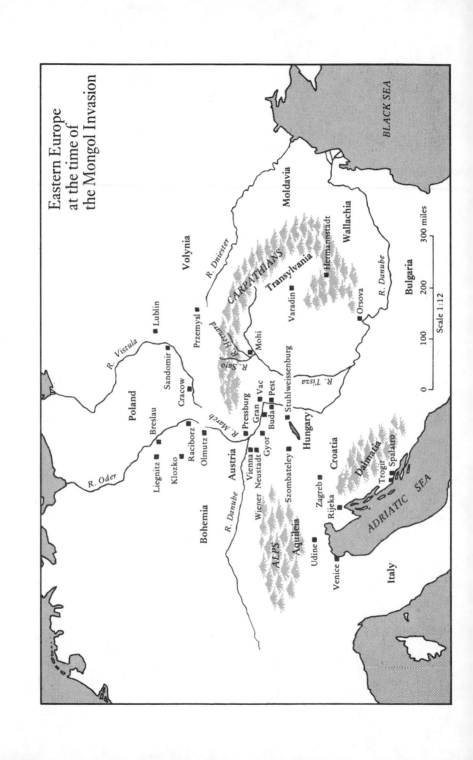

Eastern Europe
at the time of
the Mongol Invasion

BLACK SEA

Moldavia

Volynia

R. Dniester

CARPATHIANS

Transylvania

Wallachia

Hermannstadt

Varadin

Orsova

R. Danube

Bulgaria

Lublin

Przemysl

R. Vistula

Sandomir

Cracow

Poland

Breslau

Liegnitz

Klozko

Raciborz

Olmutz

R. Oder

Bohemia

R. March

Pressburg

Gran

Vac

Buda

Pest

Stuhlweissenburg

Mohi

R. Sajo

R. Hernad

R. Tisza

Hungary

Austria

Vienna

Wiener Neustadt

Gyor

Szombateley

R. Danube

ALPS

Aquileia

Zagreb

Croatia

Rijeka

Udine

Venice

Italy

Dalmatia

Trogir

Spalatro

ADRIATIC SEA

Scale 1:12

0   100   200   300 miles

7
The Invasion of Europe Begins

FOR at least two years before the Mongol armies crossed the Carpathians, all the European rulers were aware of their intentions. In France, Germany and England the plunderers of Russia became known as the 'Tartars' after Friar Julian, inspired by the legend of Gog and Magog and the Russian name 'Tatar', had introduced the word in his Latin report, referring to them as 'Tartari', the people from hell. But the only ruler who believed that they intended to carry out their threats was King Bela IV of Hungary.

The first western country to be affected by the Russian campaign was England. Every year ships from the countries around the Baltic used to sail to Yarmouth to buy the rich herring catch, but in 1238 the people of Novgorod and its dependencies, who were preparing for the return of the Mongols and repelling the lesser incursions by opportunists in the west, kept their ships at home, while the ships from Sweden, Gotland and the Livonian coast were being used to transport the invading armies of Earl Birger and the Livonian Knights. Consequently no ships came to England that year. There was a glut on the herring market, merchants went bankrupt and even deep inland fifty pickled herrings could be bought for a shilling.

In the same year the source of the first appeals for help was even more surprising. While Batu was conquering Russia, other Mongol armies were extending their empire beyond Khwarizm in the Middle East, and since the conciliatory policies of the Holy Roman Emperor Frederick II had led to an uneasy peace between Christendom and Islam, the Saracen princes, who found themselves facing a far greater threat than the crusades, turned to Europe for support. Not only Frederick, but also King Louis IX of France and King Henry III of England received Moslem ambassadors, of whom the most notorious were the representatives of the sinister 'Old Man of the Mountains' who commanded the Ismaili 'Order of the Assassins'. But the emperor, Frederick II, and his armies were preparing for the culmination of a violent struggle with the papacy, and the attitude of the rest of Christendom was epitomized in the reaction of Peter des Roches, Bishop of Winchester: 'Let us leave these dogs to devour one another that they may all be consumed and perish; and we when we proceed against the enemies of Christ who remain, will slay them and cleanse the face of the earth, so that all the world will be subject to the one Catholic Church and there will be one shepherd and one fold.'

Unfortunately the appeals and the warnings that came out of Hungary fell on equally deaf ears. Friar Julian's reports and the threats contained in Batu's letter were passed on to the Holy Roman Emperor and to Salvio Salvi, Bishop of Perugia, who was the papal legate in Hungary. But although the pope, who was delighted by the destruction of the schismatic Russians, was genuinely anxious at the prospect of an invasion in powerful Catholic Hungary, he was in no position to help since he needed every Christian soldier he could muster to defend himself against the Holy Roman Emperor. The emperor for his part, who was equally preoccupied, would have been even less likely to help Hungary than he would have been to help the Saracens since he resented the recent withdrawal of Hungarian support for his cause, after King Bela had discovered that some of his rebellious barons had gone to Vienna to offer the emperor his crown. Besides, Frederick believed that the Mongols were already too fully absorbed by their new conquests and too far from their base to be dangerous. He also had received a letter from Batu demanding the surrender of the empire and offering him a position in the Mongol hierarchy, but he had only joked about it, saying that with his experience he was well qualified for the post of the khan's falconer.

In a conservative, reactionary and superstitious age, Frederick II stood out as a progressive and enlightened despot. The grandson of Frederick Barbarossa and King Roger II of Sicily, he had been brought up in Palermo as a proud Sicilian. He spoke Latin, Greek, Italian, French and Arabic; he had a passion for scientific experiment; he had studied astronomy; and he was also an accomplished falconer and an erudite ornithologist. Since his scholarship had led him to look upon his European contemporaries with arrogant contempt and reject their backward traditions, his reason and his curiosity had led him to reach out towards the superior world of Islam and regard its princes as his only cultural and intellectual equals. His Moslem mercenaries and his harem so scandalized the prudish and newly ascetic Christian clergy, against whose attempts to extend their temporal power he was an implacable enemy, that they gave him the nickname '*Stupor Mundi*'.

The clergy had returned to open demonstrations of poverty and simplicity in an attempt to regain the hearts of the common people and win their support for Pope Innocent III's campaign to persuade their princes, who ruled by divine right, to accept God's representative on earth as at least their nominal overlord. Frederick, however, was determined to recover the Sicilian domains in northern Italy which had been naïvely ceded to the papacy as a result of this policy. Against Frederick's efforts Pope Honorius III, who succeeded Innocent III, could do little more than protest, since he needed Frederick to take part in a crusade. But although Frederick promised to lead a crusade as early as 1215, every year for the next five years he postponed his departure with a plausible excuse until the pope was prepared to proclaim him Holy Roman Emperor, to which he was entitled as the grandson of Frederick Barbarossa. Eventually the pope gave in and Frederick was crowned, but for the next seven years he still managed to avoid the crusade. In 1227 Honorius was succeeded by Gregory IX, a much stronger man, and when Frederick embarked for the Holy Land and then turned back on the pretext that his crew were sick, Gregory excommunicated him.

Frederick was left with no alternative. The excommunication would be grounds for disobedience among the princes in his German domains to whom he had granted a dangerous amount of autonomy in order to win their support. In June 1228 he set out on a crusade against his friend the Sultan of Egypt, who only the year before had presented him with a giraffe for his menagerie, the first ever to be seen in Europe.

While Frederick was away, Pope Gregory hoped to bring about his downfall by taking over the disputed Italian territories with his own mercenaries and setting up an alternative king in Germany, but the emperor and the sultan conceived a contemptuous ruse by which Frederick would appear to succeed without a drop of Christian or Moslem blood being shed, and within a year Frederick had returned, having acquired Jerusalem, Bethlehem and Nazareth on a ten-year lease from the sultan. The pope's mercenaries were driven out of Lombardy, but the ensuing treaty of San Germano, by which Frederick was accepted back into the Catholic church, did nothing to settle the territorial disputes. After decisively crushing an uprising in Lombardy at the battle of Cortenuova in 1237, Frederick reasserted his suzerainty over Spoleto and Ancona, declared his intention of making Rome his capital and began to canvass support from France and England. Horrified, Pope Gregory riposted by excommunicating him again and summoning a great council of all Christendom to meet in Rome at Easter 1241, to plan a united crusade against the infidel emperor. If this council were to secure enough support, it would be a threat not only to Frederick's ambitions in Italy, but also to his future as emperor, and so, while King Bela was desperately pleading for help, Frederick was preparing to march on Rome and prevent the council from meeting. Meanwhile the pope was also preparing to defend himself.

It was this struggle between empire and papacy that must bear the greatest responsibility for Europe's inability to present a united front against the Mongols. The armies in the front lines, the Teutonic Knights, the Poles, the Hungarians and the Bulgars, were isolated and unsupported, and the Mongols knew it.

Founded in 1198, the Order of the Teutonic Knights of Saint Mary's Hospital in Jerusalem did not remain in the Middle East to compete with the two older orders of knights, the Templars and the Hospitallers. The kingdoms of Islam were not the only areas of the world where the conquest of land and the acquisition of other men's wealth could be justified as dissemination of the true Christian faith and dignified by the title of a crusade, and soon after their foundation the Teutonic Knights began to concentrate their attentions on northern Europe. For a time they settled in Hungary, where King Bela's father, Andreas II, gave them land in return for their military services against the Cumans. But when the Cumans and the Hungarian crown became reconciled after the first Mongol attack in 1222, they were thrown out and moved on to northern Prussia and Lithuania on the Baltic coast. They then absorbed the Sword Brethren who had already settled there, conquered the indigenous pagan tribes and established themselves in large independent estates, which, in recognition of the papal policy, they held in fief from the Holy See. The extent of their estates, and their prospects for increasing them, soon attracted many more of the German nobles to whom the membership of their brotherhood of knights was limited. While the Holy Roman Empire and the papacy were at war, they managed to continue their unrestrained expansion by diplomatically remaining on equally good terms with both the empire, in which their *hochmeister* was a prince, and the papacy, from which they held their right of tenure. By 1240 they had become a major military power and were preparing to carry the 'True Cross' into the lands of the schismatic Russians, and incidentally acquire for themselves the fabled riches of Novgorod. In time, their white cloaks and tunics, decorated with a black cross, were to become as great a symbol of 'imperialist oppression' to the people of Russia as the yak-tailed standards of the Mongols.

The Teutonic Knights built ports along the Baltic coast, through which a regular flow of German peasants and craftsmen travelled inland to farm the new estates and build the great castles that would defend them. And as the estates grew and flourished, their southern neighbour Conrad, ruler of the Polish province of Mazovia, looked on with embarrassed apprehension. Constantly threatened by the brutally savage pagan tribes in Prussia, he had been one of the most enthusiastic supporters of the Teutonic Knights and had even given them his province of Chelmno, which he had been unable to defend, but now the emergence of a new German power on his northern border was an even more menacing prospect than the merciless raids of the pagan tribes. Vast numbers of German immigrants from Brandenburg had been allowed to settle in the Polish province of Silesia and in the province of Great Poland, most of which had been taken over by Silesia's ruler, Henry the Bearded. It was this prince's ill-concealed ambition to see his son, Henry the Pious, crowned in Cracow as the king of a reunited Poland, and if his grateful new subjects and the sympathy-seeking Holy Roman Emperor were to persuade the Teutonic Knights to assist him in this ambition, there would be little that the other Polish dukes could do to stop them.

Since the death of King Boleslaw III in 1138, Poland, like Russia, had disintegrated into a collection of feuding principalities, Boleslaw having divided the land among his four sons, and their principalities having been further divided by later generations. By the beginning of the thirteenth century the country had collapsed into chaotic civil war, after which various royal dukes had attemped unsuccessfully to have themselves proclaimed king. At the time of the Mongol invasion there were still nine separate principalities, each with its own jealous aristocracy and ecclesiastical hierarchy, which had again been consolidated under the rule of four dukes: Conrad of Mazovia; Miecislaw of Oppeln; Conrad's nephew Boleslaw the Chaste of Sandomir, who also controlled Cracow and claimed the title of king; and the most powerful, Henry the Pious of Silesia, who had succeeded his father in 1238 and successfully defended his province of Lubsz against an attempted take over by Brandenburg and Magdeburg. Two of these dukes were related to King Bela of Hungary: Henry was his cousin and Boleslaw had married his daughter Kunigunda. But although Bela had warned them of the inevitable consequences of the fall of Russia, he had failed to communicate his dread of the Mongols, and even Conrad had been unmoved by the disasters that had befallen Prince Michael of Chernigov, who had taken refuge with him before moving on to Silesia. In Poland, the sudden appearance of Baidar and Kadan's army came as a devastating surprise.

In the few years since his accession to the throne of Hungary, Bela IV's position had been severely weakened by his own deter-mined attempts to restore the dignity and authority of the crown. Throughout the reign of his profligate and capricious father, he had openly condemned him for his irresolute deference to his barons and the extravagance of his injudicious favouritism. Bela was by nature serious and pedantic, but his father's continued self-deception and constant contempt for his company had made him cynical and aloof, and for a long time he had been bitter: at the age of seven he had witnessed the murder of his mother by barons who objected to her lavish retinue, and then seen his father marry again without even attempting to bring the culprits to justice. By the time he came to the throne in 1235, at the age of twenty-nine, his resolve to redeem the crown's prestige and replenish its treasury had hardened into an obsession and the reforms and retributions began at once. He confiscated estates that had been given to worth-less favourites; in a symbolic ceremony he burned all the chairs in the council chamber, and did not replace them, so that in future his councillors would have to stand in his presence; and he arrested his father's corrupt treasurer and put out his eyes. His obviously sincere interest in the prosperity of his kingdom earned him a worthy and reliable body of support, but the majority of his barons, fearing the loss of the freedoms that they had been granted by the Golden Bull in 1222 (an equivalent to the English *Magna Carta*), opposed him, and without their consent he could not hope to raise anything like the full strength of his celebrated army.

It is not surprising, therefore, that he welcomed the Cumans with such enthusiasm, but the Cuman settlement was a failure. The Hungarians regarded the sudden and enormous increase in the immigrant population with suspicion. Most of the Hungarian steppe had become farmland and was no longer suitable for nomad herdsmen, and when the crops between the Danube and the Tisza, where the Cumans had settled, were trampled by their horses, it was seen as justification for a nationwide protest, expressing all the usual prejudices: the Cuman camps were filthy; their cooking was foul-smelling; and their idle and barbarous menfolk were a threat to the honour of Hungarian women.

Eager for popular support, the barons took up the cause and pressed for the Cumans' expulsion, but Bela was adamant. He was building forts and barricades with the pine trees in the Carpathian passes, and he intended to garrison them with his own standing army. If these fell, the Cuman cavalry would be his only line of defence against the Mongols until self-preservation forced the barons to rally. His neighbours had not offered him an alliance. The Holy Roman Emperor had ignored him, and so desperate was the pope that while Bela was trying to recruit his subjects to fight in their own defence, the pope's representatives were recruiting them for a crusade, not against the Mongols or the Saracens, but against the Holy Roman Emperor.

Soon after Christmas 1240 Bela's scouts began to come in with regular reports that the Mongols were advancing. Early in the new year he rode up to the Carpathians to inspect the fortifications and placed their garrisons under the command of Nador Denes, the leader of his council. When he returned, he ordered a general mobilization and summoned all the barons and bishops, who had their own military retainers, to attend a council of war at Buda on 17 February 1241. The barons may not have been quite as oblivious to the danger as they pretended, on the appointed day the majority of the army was assembled, including Kotian and his Cumans. But although the barons were willing to muster their soldiers, they were not prepared to lead them into battle without reward. They argued that Bela had brought the invasion on himself by declaring his support for the Russian princes who had once been his enemies, and they were convinced that the Cumans were a Mongol fifth column who would turn against them as soon as the invasion began. Bela compromised and placed Kotian and the other Cuman leaders under house arrest as hostages for the Cumans' loyalty, but still the barons refused to fight without more privileges and greater autonomy, and Bela was not prepared to give in to the sort of blackmail that had eroded the royal power during the reign of his father. The stalemate continued even after 10 March, when a messenger arrived with the news that the Mongols were attacking the Carpathian passes, and while Bela pleaded and the barons resisted, the Hungarian army stood by, ready, waiting and idle.

Bela dispatched yet another letter begging for assistance from the Duke of Austria, Frederick II, but although this time the duke set out at once with a small army, his motive was selfish curiosity rather than any desire to help his neighbour. Like his namesake the Holy Roman Emperor, the Duke of Austria (who was to be known by several nicknames including Frederick the Valiant, Frederick the Warlike and, most appropriately, Frederick the Quarrelsome) had also been offered the Hungarian crown by rebellious barons in the last year of the reign of Bela's feeble father, and to prevent him taking it by force Andreas and Bela had made a pre-emptive strike with an enormous army which reached the gates of Vienna and only withdrew after Frederick had bought them off with a crippling payment of gold. His consequent fear of the Hungarian army and his war with King Wenceslas of Bohemia, which had recently been ended by the threat of a Mongol invasion in Poland, had prevented him from taking his revenge and annexing the coveted Hungarian *departments* on the west of the Danube, but the possibility of Bela's defeat at the hands of what he believed to be no more than a horde of nomad raiders presented a welcome opportunity for the achievement of his ambition.

On 14 March a grimy and battered Nador Denes arrived in Buda. The Carpathian passes had fallen, his garrisons had been annihilated and the Mongols were advancing into Hungary.

Bela sent his wife to safety in Austria, charging Bishop Stephen of Vac to escort her as far as the border, and persuaded the barons to move the army across the Danube from the fortress of Buda on the high west bank to the German settlement of Pest on the lower east bank, but only the Cumans rode forward to stand in the way of the Mongol advance.

His scouts had been so inefficient that he still did not realize the full extent of the danger. All he knew was that an army had entered northern Hungary, but in January and February the southern wing of the Mongol army under Subedei and Kuyuk had ravaged Moldavia and Wallachia and while Kuyuk had forced the Oitosch pass into the mountains of Transylvania, Subedei had entered by the Mehedia pass in the far south and stormed Orsova. Transylvania and south-eastern Hungary had already suffered the same terror as eastern Russia. Towns had been burned, citizens slaughtered, churches pillaged and women raped. The king's silver mines at Rodna had been destroyed and at one town, Varadin, the Mongols had been forced to abandon their camp because of the stench from rotting corpses. There had not been time for most of the Transylvanian barons and bishops to bring their armies to Buda and it was Kuyuk's job to keep them occupied while Subedei advanced north behind them. By mounting dummies on his spare horses he had convinced them that his strength was far greater than it actually was, and they were now assembling to defend themselves at Hermannstadt while Subedei was racing up the Tisza to join Batu. Meanwhile, Batu's main army, which had taken the Verecke pass where Nador Denes had been in command, was advancing on Pest at such a speed that his vanguard is said to have come down from the mountains through the snow at the rate of sixty miles per day, and on 17 March the right wing under Siban attacked Vac, only twenty miles north of Pest. The whole of Hungary east of the Danube was in the grip of a Mongol pincer.

Bela's relations with his army continued to deteriorate. When Vac fell and its population was slaughtered, the impatient Archbishop Hugolin of Calocsa rode out to challenge Siban and returned with only his personal retinue, after his entire command had been lured into a marsh and slaughtered. The loyal barons and the contingent of Templars who had been posted to Hungary joined the archbishop in blaming Bela for not supporting him. When the Duke of Austria arrived discord developed into catastrophe.

Frederick took up the cause of the barons who were refusing to

fight without reward, and made similar demands for himself, saying that he had brought with him evidence to support their preju-
dice against the Cumans. His Austrian army had captured one of
Siban's patrols; the officers were Mongols, but some of the men
were Cumans who had been conscripted in Russia. This, he maintained, was proof that the Cumans were untrustworthy, although
he knew the truth. Having gained the support of the dissident
barons, he set about winning the hearts of their soldiers by chal-
lenging two of the Mongols to single combat, running one through
with his spear and slicing off the other's arm with a single blow
from his sword.

When Bela still refused to expel the only soldiers who were
standing in the way of the advancing enemy, some of the barons
crossed the Danube by night and broke into the house in Buda
where Kotian and the other Cuman princes were being held.
Realizing what was about to happen, Kotian killed his wives and
then committed suicide while the other princes were defending
themselves; and to please the jeering crowd that had gathered
outside, the barons cut off all their heads and threw them into the
street. When the news reached their camp the Cumans went wild
with fury. They attacked and slaughtered the soldiers of the Bishop
of Czanad who were marching to join Bela at Pest and the bishop
himself only escaped because he was so sick that he had to be
carried in a litter and had been taken to safety as soon as the
fighting began. The Cumans rode towards Austria devastating the
countryside and sacking several cities including Szombateley and
then turned south and disappeared into Bulgaria carrying all their
plunder with them.

Through their own treachery the Hungarians had lost their most
valuable allies and, satisfied that he had done as much damage as he
could, Frederick collected his soldiers and marched back to
Austria on the pretext that Bela was being unreasonable.

By the end of March Subedei and Siban had joined forces with
Batu and the Mongol army was drawn up in front of Pest, but Bela
kept his nerve and still steadfastly refused to make any concessions
to his barons. If they remained they would have no choice but to
defend themselves in the inevitable attack, and many were preparing to abandon Bela when suddenly the Mongol army turned
round and rode away. The invaders had obviously decided that the
army assembled in Pest was too strong for them, and since victory

now seemed possible, the dissidents at last agreed to join the loyal barons and the Templars who were already clamouring for pursuit. If it looked as though Bela was going to be defeated they could still abandon him, and if he was going to be victorious, it would be best for them to have shared in the glory.

On 7 April 1241 King Bela of Hungary ordered his army of a hundred thousand men to advance in pursuit of the retreating Mongols.

8
The Fury of the Tartars

WHILE Batu's army was advancing into Hungary, Baidar and Kadan were marching through Poland. In February 1241 they entered the territory of Lublin, burning the cities of Lublin and Zawichost and laying waste the countryside. They were moving slowly and yet, after crossing the frozen Vistula on the ice, they were able to sack Sandomir, which was defended by no more than a normal garrison, and pause to plunder its Cistercian monastery without being threatened by a relieving army. The Poles had obviously been taken by complete surprise. With no apparent opposition, the conditions seemed ideal for a quick conquest, but unfortunately Baidar and Kadan's objective was to draw the northern European armies away from Hungary, and it did not yet look as though these armies had even been mobilized. Although their own army was already dangerously small, they decided to divide it and spread alarm over as wide an area as possible; in the last resort Mongols could always retreat faster than any European army could advance. While Kadan rode north-west to attack Mazovia, Baidar took a calculated risk and continued his advance south-west, directly towards the Polish capital at Cracow.

Raiding and burning and drawing attention to itself, Baidar's vanguard advanced to within a few miles of Cracow and then slowly turned back as though returning to its camp with its plunder and its prisoners. Vladimir, the Palatine of Sandomir and Cracow, who commanded the armies of Boleslaw the Chaste, rode out of the city in considerable strength and attacked. The Mongols broke and fled and the prisoners escaped, but Vladimir had given himself away. Boleslaw's army would be one of the first to march to the rescue of his father-in-law, the King of Hungary, and Baidar had not only found it, but had lured it out from behind the city walls where it might have held out long enough for the other Polish dukes to reach Hungary unopposed or to come to its relief in dangerously superior numbers. When the Mongols did not re-appear the soldiers of Sandomir and Cracow, believing that the raiders were on the run, began to advance and on 18 March at Chmielnik, only eleven miles from Cracow, Baidar ambushed them. Vladimir and most of his soldiers died in a hail of Mongol arrows.

As the battle was drawing to a close, a Mongol reconnaissance unit approached Cracow. Fugitives from the battlefield had already passed through, and Boleslaw and his family had left for Hungary with all the treasure they could carry. While the citizens were preparing to abandon the city and take refuge in the forests, a trumpeter continued to sound the alarm until a Mongol arrow struck him down. When the main body of the Mongol army arrived, Cracow was deserted, and on 24 March it was burned. To this day the disaster is commemorated: every hour on the hour, a trumpeter from the Cracow fire department sounds the call from the four corners of the cathedral tower, but the call is never finished, it splutters abruptly to an end just at the moment when the Mongol arrow struck the look-out.

Baidar and Kadan had arranged to meet again at Breslau, the capital of Silesia, where they expected to find the strongest of the Polish armies, and since the bridges on the river Oder had been destroyed, Baidar had first to collect all the boats at Raciborz and build his own pontoon bridge. By the time he reached Breslau, the citizens had already burned their own city and retired into the citadel. Kadan had not yet arrived and Baidar began to lay siege to it, but at last he received a report that Henry of Silesia had assembled an army of the northern princes at Liegnitz, which was only forty miles away, and King Wenceslas of Bohemia was march-ing to join him. Baidar abandoned the siege, sent word to Kadan and Batu, and set out at full speed to reach Liegnitz before Wenceslas.

The people of Breslau believed that they had been saved by a miracle, and the legend grew that the prayers of the prior of the Dominican monastery had brought down upon him such a radiant light from heaven that the Mongols had fled in terror.

At Liegnitz, now known as Legnica, Henry's hastily assembled army numbered no more than twenty-five thousand men and many of them were untrained and ill-equipped. Miecislaw of Oppeln had brought his army and the Margrave of Moravia had sent an army under the command of his son Boleslaw, but they were mostly made up of the usual inexperienced feudal levies. Many of the conscripts from Great Poland and the large contingent of volunteers assembled by the Bavarian gold miners from Goldburg in Silesia were armed with no more than the tools of their trades. The detachments of the Knights Templar from France and the Hospitallers were too small to be of any consequence. Apart from Henry's own army of mercenaries and regular Silesian soldiers, who were both experienced and distinguished, the only other formidable unit in the combined army was the splendid contingent of Teutonic Knights led by their Prussian *landmeister*, Poppo von Osterna. The morale of the ignorant conscripts was raised by the confidence and magnificence of the Christian knights with their banners and their fine armour, but although these conscripts might have been fiercely courageous defenders on the city walls, it was hopeless to imagine that they could be effective on a battlefield.

After pillaging large areas of Mazovia and defeating one or two detachments of Conrad's army, Kadan joined Baidar on the road to Leignitz. On 9 April 1241 Henry rode out of the city to meet them, not knowing that Wenceslas with his army of fifty thousand men was only one day's march away. As he passed the church of Saint Mary a stone fell from the roof and nearly struck his head; it was recorded as an ill omen. On the plain beyond the city, in a place that was afterwards known as Walstadt (the chosen place), he drew up his army in four divisions: the volunteers from Goldburg under Boleslaw Syepiolka; the conscripts from Great Poland and a few survivors from Cracow under Sudislaw, the brother of the Palatine Vladimir who had died at Chmielnik; the army from Oppeln and the Teutonic Knights under Duke Miecislaw; and in the centre the Silesian and Moravian armies with the Templars and the Hospitallers under Henry's own command. When the Mongol vanguard advanced in close order it seemed so small that Henry sent only his Silesian cavalry to meet it, but when the Silesians fell back after the first volley of arrows, he sent in the horsemen from Great Poland under Sudislaw and the Duke of Oppeln's cavalry with the Teutonic Knights. The Mongols began to retreat, but the reinforcements had not been enough to break their ranks, so Henry himself advanced with the Templars and Hospitallers, committing the last of his cavalry. While the Mongol reserves of light cavalry advanced to their positions on either flank, the vanguard, which had been a *mangudai*, broke and fled. As soon as the front and flanks of the disorganized mass of Henry's pursuing cavalry came under the full fire of the Mongol archers, smoke bombs were let off across their rear, screening them from the rest of the army, and once the Mongol heavy cavalry had moved in for the final blow, the archers rode through the smoke screen and shot down the helpless infantry. The allied army was routed. The Prussian *landmeister* escaped but most of his Teutonic Knights, together with the Polish aristocracy and the flower of northern Europe's chivalry, lay dead on the battlefield. Ponce d'Aubon, Grand Master of the French Templars, later wrote to King Louis, reporting the total loss of their small detachment: nine brothers, three knights, two sergeants and five hundred men-at-arms. After the battle the Mongols recorded the number of enemy dead by cutting an ear from every body and collecting them into nine large sacks which they sent to Batu.

Duke Henry attempted to escape with only three bodyguards, but a group of Mongols set out after him, shooting down the guards one by one, and when his exhausted horse collapsed beneath him, he tried to run in his armour until the Mongol horsemen caught up with him. The Mongols cut off his head and carried it on a spear round the walls of the citadel of Liegnitz, where the people had taken refuge after following the example of Breslau and burning their city. After the victors had gone, his wife searched the field for his body to take it away for burial at Breslau. When she found it, it had been stripped and so mutilated that she could only identify it because Henry had six toes on his left foot.

When the news of the defeat reached him, Wenceslas fell back to collect reinforcements from Thurignia and Saxony. At Klozko the Mongol vanguard found him, but his army was far too powerful for it and it was driven off by his cavalry. The vanguard returned and reported the engagement, and Baidar and Kadan, whose casualties at Liegnitz had been heavy, realized that they did not have the strength to face him. However, he was already two hundred and fifty miles from Bela's army in Hungary and all they had to do was keep him there. They made a feint advance towards the west, drawing Wenceslas after them, and then broke up into small groups and rode round him through Moravia, burning towns as they went. Within a month they had crossed into Hungary.

The Silesian and Moravian towns were so depopulated that after the war they had to be resettled with German immigrants and given tax immunity and other privileges to revive their economies. If it had not been for the many forests and marshes in which fugitives were too difficult to find, the slaughter of peasants and farmers would have made the depopulation complete.

Stupefied and shattered, the Poles were unable to understand what had happened to them. They knew nothing about the Mongols or their purpose, and from the events of the three terrible months they began to deduce their own version of the campaign and embellish it with propaganda. Confused reports of the smoke screen at Liegnitz and the strong-smelling incense which the Mongols burned beneath their standards were combined into a theory that the allies had been subjected to some form of fiendish gas attack. As always, the incredible mobility of the Mongol army had made the Poles assess its strength at five times greater than it was, and its sudden withdrawal allowed them to believe that their dauntless resistance had inflicted so many casualties that the Mongols had been forced to abandon an invasion. Forever after the battle of Liegnitz, seven noble families from Silesia and Moravia wore the Mongol cap as a mark of their ancestors' presence at what they remembered as a pyrrhic victory. Bewildered chroniclers made up names for the Mongol commanders (Baidar, for example, was known as Peta) and as time went by they recorded the universally accepted reports of allied victories in battles that had never taken place, adding to the impression that the Mongols had been driven out of Poland. Records of two of these spurious victories were used in a famous nineteenth-century forgery, the 'Koniginhofer manuscript', but it is now certain that Wenceslas never met, let alone defeated, the main body of the Mongol army, and the report of a victory by Yaroslaw of Sternburg in an attack on Olmutz, where Baidar was supposed to have been killed, is merely a misrepresentation of a raid made by the Hungarians and the Cumans in 1253. Nevertheless, several serious histories of central Europe still refer to Liegnitz as a Polish victory, and the most widespread misunderstanding, caused by the use of nicknames and the awesome difficulty encountered in translating oriental characters, has managed to survive into the majority of general history books today. Kadan was mistranslated as Kaidu, and it is therefore said that it was Ogedei's grandson Kaidu, and not his son Kadan, who partnered Baidar in Poland in 1241. Quite apart from the obscurity of the manuscripts this is impossible since it is known that Kaidu was born in 1230 and ten-year-old boys did not command Mongol armies.

While Baidar and Kadan had been sweeping through Poland, Batu's armies had been advancing into Hungary, and once Baidar and Kadan had located the armies of Silesia and Bohemia and were preparing to secure the northern flank by eliminating or decoying them, Batu, who had been taunting Bela's soldiers in Pest, began to withdraw. As always the co-ordination of the Mongol armies was faultless, but the timing of the decisive engagements was astonishing. It can not be dismissed as coincidence, and since the uncertainty of the enemy positions would have made pre-planning impossible, the only explanation seems to be the speed of the Mongol messengers and in particular the efficiency of their signalling system. The day after the destruction of the Silesian army at Liegnitz, the southern flank was secured by Kuyuk who stormed Hermannstadt, over five hundred miles away, and destroyed the army of Transylvania, and in the centre Batu and Subedei halted to engage Bela on the heath at Mohi, which lies south-west of the river Sajo just before it joins the Tisza.

During the retreat Subedei, Mangku and Batu rode ahead of their soldiers to inspect the battlefield which Batu had chosen. On the afternoon of 10 April the Mongol army rode over the heath, crossed the Sajo by the only bridge and continued ten miles beyond it into the thickets, with the hills and vineyards of Tokay ahead of them and the rivers Tisza and Hernard on either side. In the evening when Bela arrived, a reconnaissance of a thousand Hungarian horsemen crossed the stone bridge, rode into the thickets, found nothing and returned to guard the bridge while the remainder of their army made its camp on the heath. Hundreds of wagons were drawn up in a circle around the tents and held together with chains and ropes. In the last light of the day Batu led his staff corps back to a hilltop and showed them the Hungarian position. On their right were the marshes of the Tisza, ahead of them the Sajo, and on their left and behind them the hills and forests of Lomnitz and Diosgyor. If they could be kept on the heath, the enemy were trapped like cattle in a corral.

When night came Subedei led thirty thousand men through the hills and back to the Sajo beyond the heath. His plan was to cross over and take the enemy in the rear while Batu engaged their front, and he began to build a wooden bridge between the villages of Girines and Nady Czeks. Bela's scouts had already proved themselves to be inept on several occasions, including that afternoon, and if there were any pickets they saw and heard nothing.

Just before dawn Batu launched his attack on the stone bridge. The guards held the west bank until reinforcements came from their camp and when it seemed as though the deep ranks of defenders could hold out indefinitely against a narrow column of Mongol cavalry, they jeered at them across the river. But Batu brought up a battery of seven catapults and began to bombard the far side of the bridge, 'to the accompaniment of thunderous noise and flashes of fire'. As the disordered Hungarian ranks drew back from the fire bombs and grenades, the catapults increased their range and Batu's soldiers crossed the bridge safely behind a 'rolling barrage'.

At first the Hungarians were confused by the tactical use of artillery on the battlefield, but on the heath Batu's forty thousand men faced the entire Hungarian army and it seemed only a matter of time before superior numbers would prevail. Committed to a plan which limited their ability to manoeuvre, the Mongol soldiers moved round slowly towards the centre of the heath so that the Hungarian rear would be towards Subedei's surprise attack, and only their fire power saved them from being overwhelmed by the massed charges of the finest cavalry in Europe. After two ferocious hours Batu's dangerously depleted ranks began to stretch out audaciously into a half circle as though they believed that they could surround their enemy, and as the Hungarians were preparing to charge through the line, another half circle under Subedei appeared behind them. The rest of the Mongol army had arrived at last, and the two lines closed in behind a shower of arrows. Surprised and about to be surrounded, the Hungarians had lost the advantage, but were too experienced to panic. Before the circle could be completed, they formed into columns and made an orderly withdrawal into their fortified camp.

The Mongols surrounded the camp, but Batu was despondent. The second bridge had taken longer than expected to build and the delay had cost him terrible casualties for which he blamed Subedei. He was no longer confident that his exhausted soldiers were strong enough to storm the camp or hold their own if the Hungarians came out again, and he wanted to play safe and retreat. Subedei, however, had more faith in his soldiers and their trust in him was absolute. 'If the princes wish to retreat they may do so,' he said, 'but for my part I am resolved not to return until I have reached Pest and the Danube'.

The battle continued, and in the Hungarian camp many of the barons, who had earlier fought valiantly when victory seemed certain, would have abandoned Bela to his fate, if their camp had not already been surrounded. Bela's brother Koloman rallied enough men to charge the Mongol artillery which was pounding the camp with fire bombs, but they were driven back. Then, after a bombardment of several hours had wrecked the fortifications, burned most of the tents and destroyed the Hungarian morale, the Mongol army began to mass for a charge, leaving a large gap in their lines in front of the gorge through which the armies had entered the heath on the day before. A few Hungarian horsemen made a run for it and escaped through the gap, and when the Mongol charge began, only the Templars and the soldiers of Koloman and Archbishop Hugolin formed up in a wedge to meet it. As Subedei had hoped, the remainder, many of them throwing down their arms and their armour to lessen the weight for their horses, set out after the first fugitives to make their escape while the Mongols were concentrating on their attack. The soldiers in the Hungarian wedge were decimated by Mongol arrows and finally smashed by a charge of heavy cavalry under Siban. Once again, as their brothers had done two days before at Liegnitz, the Templars died to a man. Archbishop Hugolin was killed and Koloman, fatally wounded, escaped with a few survivors to join Bela and the other fugitives.

But the escape route had been a trap. When the runaway column was stretched out over the heath and through the gorge, Mongol light cavalry attacked and rode along either side of it, shooting down the fugitives as though they were hunting them. The heath became a mass of riderless horses and for thirty miles beyond it the road back to Pest was littered with Hungarian dead, 'like stones in a quarry'. What had begun as a fierce contest between two extraordinary armies had ended in a rout, and the most conservative estimate of the Hungarian dead was sixty thousand men.

Only those who had been at the head of the fugitives or had ridden through the chaos into the hills at the side of the gorge

escaped, and among these were Bela and Koloman. Bela outran his
Mongol pursuers by taking a fresher horse from one of his loyal
followers each time his own tired, and when he was clear he
doubled back, swam over the Sajo and spent the night among the
trees, guarded only by an old Slav retainer called Vochu. Koloman
reached the Danube, crossing in a boat with the women and
children who were fleeing from Pest, and made his way to his own
Hungarian domains in Croatia where he died of his wounds.

The Mongols advanced, burned Pest and rode north and south
along the Danube, terrifying the citizens of Buda on the western
bank, although they did not cross. Instead they began to consolidate their conquest of eastern Hungary and to destroy Bela's
chances of rallying its inhabitants. In the camp at Mohi they had
captured the great seal of the Hungarian chancellor and they used
it to issue a fake proclamation which prevented the mustering of a
new army: 'Do not fear the rage and ferocity of these dogs; do not
leave your houses; we have only been surprised and we shall soon
with God's help recapture our camp; continue to pray to God to
assist us in the destruction of our enemies.' In the cities they
minted new coins which made Bela's currency worthless and in the
country they persuaded the farmers to return to their land under
Mongol protection.

Through the Carpathian mountains Bela and Vochu made their
way towards Austria where Bela believed he would find refuge.
One night they sheltered in a monastery in Thurocz where Bela
met a fellow fugitive, Boleslaw the Chaste, who had fled from
Cracow. At Pressburg on the Austrian border Bela was reunited
with his wife and children and naïvely accepted the hospitality of
Duke Frederick, only to find himself a prisoner. In return for his
freedom and indeed his safety, Frederick demanded the repayment
of the indemnity that he had been forced to pay six years before,
but all the wealth that Bela had with him, including the Hungarian
crown jewels, was not nearly enough. In addition he was forced to
pawn three of his western *departments*, and while Frederick's
soldiers were preparing to take over these new dominions, which
were probably the predominantly German areas of Moson, Sopron
and Vas, Bela and his family travelled south to the safety of
Croatia.

As news of the disasters in Poland and Hungary began to spread
throughout the rest of Europe, a wave of panic followed it. Grue-

some rumours of diabolical atrocities committed by unearthly monsters with supernatural powers led to a superstitious hysteria, and even the clergy revived the old myths and legends in an attempt to explain the mysterious invaders. The Dominican Ricoldo of Monte Croce argued learnedly that the true name Mongol was derived from Magogoli, the followers of Magog, and that the Tartars trembled at the name of Alexander. In Germany it was said that the Tartars were the lost tribes of Israel and that Jews were smuggling arms to them, using barrels which they pretended were filled with poisoned wine, with the result that at several border posts Jewish merchants were indiscriminately slaughtered. Mongol women were said to have accompanied the army and to have fought in battle as fiercely as the men. The Hungarians had described the invaders as 'dog-faced Tartars', probably because of the shape of their fur caps, but Ivo of Narbonne recorded that their princes had the heads of dogs and that the soldiers, who ate the bodies of the dead, tore off the breasts of the young women that they had raped and reserved them as delicacies for these princes. After the collapse of the mighty Hungarian army it seemed, even to the pope, that all of Christendom might be destroyed by these merciless horsemen from hell and every day in the crowded churches of northern Europe the congregations prayed, 'from the fury of the Tartars oh Lord deliver us'.

Many of the despondent reports which were sent to all the western princes by the leaders of the military orders and the monks in the devastated areas were equally coloured with fantastic anecdotes. Even the most accurate, addressed to Duke Henry II of Brabant and all Christians by the provincial vicar of the Franciscan in Bohemia and Poland, Friar Jordan of Giano, which gave a detailed account of the Mongols' mobility, tactics and use of artillery, also contained his own fanciful description of their merciless women. With a simile worthy of a celibate he wrote: 'She who fights best is regarded as the most desirable, just as in our country she who weaves and sews best is more desired than the one who is beautiful.'

Friar Jordan's report, together with a call to arms from the Count of Lorraine, was passed on by the Duke of Brabant to the Bishop of Paris, but his French king was already preparing for the Mongol onslaught with the resignation of a martyr. The king's letter from the master of the French Templars, recording the loss at Liegnitz and written without knowledge of the defeat at Mohi, had referred to the armies of Bohemia and Hungary and ended with the warning: 'If by the will of God they should be defeated, these Tartars will find no one to stand against them as far as your land.' When his mother, Queen Blanche, asked him what was to be done, Louis simply replied: 'We have this consolation from Heaven, Mother. If these people whom we call Tartars come against us, either we shall send them back to Hell where they came from, or else they will send us to Heaven, where we shall enjoy the bliss that waits for the chosen.'

The chronicler Vincent of Beauvais later described how Batu had sacrificed to demons before invading Hungary and how one of these demons had sent three spirits ahead of him to destroy his enemies: the spirit of fear, the spirit of mistrust and the spirit of discord. The fable was more of an allegory than a fantasy. Instead of preparing his defences, the Duke of Austria was using his soldiers to invade the unoccupied Hungarian territories, and even now, when the fall of eastern Poland and Hungary augured the destruction of everything that they were fighting for, the pope and the emperor would not be reconciled. Frederick II blamed Bela for his incompetence and held the pope responsible for placing Christendom in jeopardy. In Italy the Bishop of Ferrara published a letter which had been smuggled to him, claiming that imperial messengers had been seen with the Tartars, and in Germany the pope's representatives spread rumours that the emperor had sent for them.

The universal terror of the Mongols offered the pope his only chance of survival. The emperor was winning the war in Italy and if his supporters could be persuaded that it was this war that left Europe disorganized and defenceless, they might force him to abandon it. The pope wrote to the three sons of Henry the Pious of Silesia, saying, 'When we consider that through these Tartars the name of Christian might utterly perish, our bones shudder at the thought', and, praising the Duke of Carinthia who had attempted to reconcile him with the emperor, he continued, 'Should he show himself worthy of peace with the Church and prepared to fulfil the conditions indispensable to the honour of God, we will gladly open the bosom of our apostolic fatherhood to him who returns full of humility.' Frederick, however, countered by sending a special embassy to the pope, 'that he might remove the many obstacles which by word and deed he has raised before us and permit us to set forth to the defence of Christendom'.

When he reached Zagreb, Bela wrote to the emperor, the pope and the King of France, pleading for amnesty and united assistance, and sent the Bishop of Vac to the emperor to offer his allegiance in return for support. But the pope answered expressing even more inflexibly what he had said to the Silesian princes, and the emperor told the Bishop of Vac that he could do no more until the pope came to terms with his ambassadors. When his embassy inevitably failed, Frederick wrote from Spoleto to King Louis claiming that he had been left with no alternative but to press on towards Rome, so that when he had been received back into the church he would be in a position to lead a crusade against the Tartars.

Amidst all the duplicity and recrimination there was one concession: the pope allowed a crusade to be preached against the Mongols in Germany and the emperor sent his thirteen-year-old son Conrad, who had been crowned as German king in 1237, to become its nominal leader. Conrad 'took the cross' at Esslingen on 19 May. Frederick composed a rousing call to arms and sent it to all the kingdoms of Europe, 'to Germany ardent in war, to France who nurses in her bosom an undaunted soldiery, to warlike Spain, to England mighty with warriors and ships, to Sicily, to savage Ireland and to frozen Norway'. Priests preached the crusade in the market places and arms and supplies were assembled in the castles. In an atmosphere of austerity, huge sums of money were collected to pay the soldiers and it was forbidden to sit in taverns or wear costly clothes.

The Duke of Austria did not join the crusade. Pretending that his soldiers were already fully engaged in the defence of his border, he wrote to Conrad on 13 June encouraging him to bring greater pressure on France, Spain and England so that they might join in the defeat of what he described as the Tartar 'hurricane'. He also invited some of the crusaders to advance through Austria at their own expense, since the enemy were massing for an attack in northern Hungary. The Mongols had indeed sent soldiers into north-western Hungary, round the corner of the Danube where it turns south after flowing from west to east through Austria, but only a reconnaissance force had crossed the Austrian border, and on the banks of the river March it had been forced to retire by a detachment of Duke Frederick's army which was advancing to attack Pressburg. In his letter Frederick reported the engagement to Conrad and claimed that his soldiers had killed three hundred of the enemy. The threat had not been enough to deter him from furthering his own ambitions in western Hungary. However, he did hope that it might persuade the crusaders to ward off an invasion while he continued to take maximum advantage of King Bela's predicament, and, apparently fearing that the skirmish might not have been enough to influence their plans, he wrote to the Bishop of Constance nine days later, exaggerating the engagement and raising the number of Mongol dead to seven hundred.

But in the unoccupied territories the Hungarians were still a match for the Austrians. In July Pressburg was successfully defended by Count Cosmos and after his capture by Count Achilles, and although Frederick's soldiers took possession of Gyor, the devastation of the countryside so incensed the local inhabitants that they burned the Austrians' camp and forced them to abandon the city.

Throughout the summer and autumn the Mongols remained beyond the Danube. Batu was anxious that his soldiers should rest and regain their strength, and he was still afraid that one defeat might lead to the loss of everything he had already gained. At a banquet at Pest, when all the princes were gathered together, he had bitterly reproached Subedei for the delay at Mohi which had cost them many casualties and one of his commanders, but Subedei had answered, 'When the Prince attacked he did not realize that where I crossed the water was deeper and my bridge was not yet ready; if he says I was late he should remember the reason', and Batu had accepted the rebuke with a new-found dignity. Honouring his commander by offering him his own cup of wine, he announced: 'Everything that we have achieved we owe to Subedei.'

During those months three of the princes, Mangku, Kuyuk and Buri, returned to Mongolia. Having reached the Danube they may have felt that they had fulfilled their obligation to Batu, and although their reasons for leaving are not recorded, those of Kuyuk and Buri are not difficult to guess: apart from their personal contempt for Batu, his growing power was a cause for envy. Mangku on the other hand was one of Batu's staunchest supporters, and he shared Batu's fear that the acceptance of Kuyuk as Ogedei's successor might lead to the creation of a hereditary dynasty among Ogedei's descendants, to the exclusion of the other imperial families. It may be that he returned to support the opposition and to keep Batu informed of the intrigues at Karakorum.

The lull created a false sense of security among Conrad's crusaders. As the summer went by their anxiety began to fade and they became indifferent to the exhortations of King Bela, who was still sending what money he could for the construction of forts on the west bank of the Danube. Eventually the crusade was postponed. The Bishop of Vac returned to Zagreb, the papal legates ordered the volunteers to remain at home and wait until they were called out against the emperor, and, before returning to their own domains, the bishops and princes took all the money that had been collected to pay the soldiers and divided it among themselves.

Meanwhile the emperor's success in Italy continued. He defeated everyone that the pope could send against him, and towards the end of August, when he was approaching Rome, old Pope Gregory died. Frederick tactfully withdrew the bulk of his army from the outskirts of the city, but while the conclave of cardinals met to elect a successor, the hall was guarded by scoffing imperial soldiers who urinated on the floor above and created such a stench in the summer heat that the English representative, Robert of Somercote, was overcome by the fumes and died. When at last the conclave agreed to a nomination that was acceptable to the Emperor, the eighty-year-old Galfrid Castiglione, who was to become Celestine IV, the old man died unconsecrated after only seventeen days and the cardinals were forced to reassemble. For nearly a year the conclave argued, the interregnum continued and the emperor's army remained in Italy.

The river Danube seldom freezes, but in the harsh winter of 1241 it froze hard, and with their usual talent for terror Batu and the main body of the Mongol army crossed over the ice on Christmas Day and attacked Gran. This cosmopolitan city, now known as Esztergom, was then the richest in Hungary and one of the leading commercial centres in eastern Europe; its archbishop was the primate of Hungary and its castle was often the residence of the king and his court. The Mongols stormed the outer city and while a battery of thirty catapults bombarded one point in the wooden walls that surrounded the old inner city, their prisoners were forced to fill the ditch beneath it with sacks of sand. The citizens set fire to the buildings, burning the warehouses that contained their merchandise and supplies, and buried all the valuable possessions that they could carry. But when the Mongols broke through the breach in the wall, new prisoners were roasted over the fires until they revealed where the treasure was hidden.

At the same time Kadan crossed from Pest, sacked Buda and advanced towards Gyor. At Stuhlweissenburg, the ancient burial place of the Hungarian kings, which was fiercely defended by a garrison of Italian mercenaries, he was forced to abandon his assault when a sudden early thaw flooded the outskirts and hampered the movements of his soldiers. The monastery of Saint Martin of Pammonia near Gyor, which had been heavily fortified by its abbot, was also allowed to survive when it withstood the first assault. There was no time to waste on protracted sieges. Even at Gran, where the castle had been gallantly defended by the Spanish burgrave, Simeon, Batu had marched on when his efforts to storm it failed. The Mongols were advancing to invade Austria.

While a reconnaissance in force crossed the Austrian border, Kadan took one *tumen* and turned south towards Zagreb to search for Bela, just as Subedei and Jebe had hunted Muhammad II twenty years before.

In preparation for the invasion the reconnaissance laid waste all the land as far as Wiener Neustadt and its scouts were seen near Klosternuburg on the northern outskirts of Vienna. Ivo of Narbonne records that this detachment laid siege to Wiener Neustadt and that it was defeated in battle by a relieving army under the command of the Dukes of Austria and Carinthia, the Patriarch of Aquileia and the Marquis of Baden. The one defeat recorded by the oriental historians, however, took place on the north of the Danube, and the only troops in the area of Wiener Neustadt at the time of the reconnaissance were the local levies. It is almost certain, therefore, that Ivo confused this reconnaissance with the force that was defeated by the Austrian duke's army the year before.

Among eight Mongol prisoners captured in Austria during this reconnaissance there was an Englishman. He had once been a Templar, but after being banished from England for an unknown crime, he had travelled through the Middle East and entered the Mongol service as an interpreter. It was said that he spoke seven languages. Matthew Paris mistakenly records that it was this

Englishman who delivered the letter to King Bela which was in fact intercepted by Friar Julian, and some say that he was in command of the reconnaissance force, but this is unlikely since such a command would not have been given to anyone other than a Mongol. The only certainty seems to be that among the many nationalities in the Mongol corps of interpreters there was at least one mysterious Englishman.

At about this time another small Mongol reconnaissance appeared outside Udine, below the Alps only sixty miles north of Venice, and the Italians began to fear that the Mongols were preparing for an invasion of Italy as well, but it was probably no more than a detachment of Kadan's army searching for King Bela. Venetian merchants had provided the Mongols' intelligence service with most of its information about the distribution of the European armies and the political allegiances of their princes, and Subedei would have been unlikely to allow an army to threaten so valuable an ally.

King Bela was hiding on the island of Rab when he heard that Kadan had already sacked Zagreb and was advancing towards the Dalmatian coast. Exchanging the defenceless island for the safety of a ship, he sailed down to Spalatro where he had established his court a few months before. The heavily-fortified city was garrisoned and so crowded with his courtiers and servants that all the squares were being used as camp sites, but Bela did not remain. Like Muhammad II he was too apprehensive to stay in one place or stand and fight, and he moved fifteen miles along the coast to the island fortress of Trogir where a ship could carry him to Italy if the Mongols attacked. At the beginning of March Kadan camped at Verbacz, thirteen miles north-east of Spalatro, and, leaving his soldiers to rest, led a reconnaissance along the coast to inspect the defences of Spalatro and Trogir. King Bela and his terrified courtiers were safer than they believed. Kadan's soldiers were exhausted and their numbers had been severely depleted by an overwhelming army of Croats who had driven them off the battlefield at Grobnok near Rijeka. His supplies had run so short that in order to make them last longer he had slaughtered all his Hungarian prisoners, and along the mountainous coast line there was no grass for his horses. Spalatro was too strong to be taken by storm and he was in no position to lay siege to it, and at Trogir, Bela could take to his ship at the first assault. To the amazement of the citizens,

Kadan's army bypassed Spalatro and rode south towards Dubrovnik.

In the north the Austrian reconnaissance returned. Only the overwhelming numbers of a combined European army could have halted the Mongol invasion and no such army existed – but the Mongol army never advanced. Europe was saved by a single act of ambitious treachery. A messenger arrived from Karakorum with the news that on 11 December 1241 Ogedei Khan had died, apparently in a sudden convulsion brought on by excessive drinking, and his wife, Toregene, was now ruling as regent until a new khan could be elected.

Throughout his short reign Ogedei had grown more and more dissipated and left the administration of his empire to his mandarin councillors. His favourite son had been Kochu, who died in 1236, and the two most distinguished of his surviving sons were Kadan and Kuyuk, although Kadan's mother had only been one of his concubines and Toregene's eldest son Kuyuk was unpopular even with his father. On the advice of his councillors, therefore, he had nominated Kochu's son Siremun as his candidate for succession. When Toregene and her family failed to change his mind in favour of Kuyuk, they encouraged his unbridled drunkenness in the hope that it would hasten his death, so that as regent Toregene would be in a position to influence the election. As time passed, however, opposition to Kuyuk had increased and when Ogedei did eventually die most of his courtiers were convinced that one of Toregene's sisters had grown tired of waiting for the wine to kill him and had put poison in it.

Toregene and her family were already preparing to achieve their ambitions: appointments in the imperial household were being given to favourites of Fatima, a Persian slave woman with whom Toregene had long been infatuated, and the mandarin councillors were being replaced by sycophantic Moslems who were prepared to buy their office with their support for Kuyuk. The invasion of Europe had to be postponed. The Mongol commanders and princes were bound by tradition to return to Karakorum for the election of a new khan and Batu was anxious to lend his support to Mangku and the other opponents of Kuyuk. Above all he knew that the regent would not allow him to retain the imperial *tumens* which made up the backbone of his army. If Kuyuk was not elected he might be able to return to Europe, and meanwhile his safest course would be to hold on to as much of his new empire as he could control with his Turkoman conscripts.

Hungary was abandoned. The Mongol army rode back across the Danube destroying everything in its path. The populations of towns and villages were slaughtered without mercy, all the barns and warehouses were systematically burned, and the already devastated *departments* of southern Hungary and Transylvania became a wilderness. Proclamations were posted in the Mongol camps declaring that all prisoners might return to their homes, but those who left were pursued and slaughtered.

Kadan had almost reached Scutari when he received the news of his father's death. Returning through Bulgaria, he joined Batu near the mouth of the Danube. Bulgaria was then a powerful kingdom, but the king, Ivan Assen II, had recently died and Kadan's raids had already been enough to shake the confidence of his successor. As Kadan's army rode through, the new king, Koloman I, paid tribute and accepted Batu as his overlord.

From the mouth of the Danube the Mongol army rode east through southern Russia towards Sarai, the base camp near the Volga, sixty miles north of Astrakhan, where Batu's brother Sinkur had been left in command. Here Batu established his capital and remained to organize the government of his new empire, while Subedei and the princes who had helped him to conquer it led the imperial *tumens* back to Mongolia. He was anxious when they left him and bitterly disappointed that his invasion of defenceless Europe had been interrupted. Yet even if Kuyuk were to be elected supreme khan, he was now powerful enough to stand alone: the plundering of Russian and European cities had made him immensely rich; his empire stretched from the Carpathians to the Urals; and nearly all the Mongol officers who had been assigned to command his Turkoman conscripts chose to remain with their new units rather than return to Mongolia. Within only a few years the city of tents at Sarai was to become an imperial capital that rivalled Karakorum, and the rich army that rode out from it was to be known as the Golden Horde.

9
The First Ambassadors

WHEN the Mongols had gone, famine and fear of the plague took their place and while the dukes of eastern Poland and the King of Hungary returned cautiously to their ruined domains, the shattered survivors of the Teutonic Knights came back from Russia to their empty castles.

In spite of their losses at Liegnitz, the Teutonic Knights had set out to take advantage of Novgorod's isolation and while the Mongols were still in Hungary they captured Pskov. Novgorod had been left without a military commander since Prince Alexander had quarrelled with the other princes and gone to live in the Mongol-occupied south, but when the city was threatened by the advance of the German crusaders, the hero who defeated the Swedes returned, and on 5 April 1242 the lightly-armed soldiers of Alexander Nevsky lured the Teutonic Knights onto the frozen surface of Lake Peipus, which broke beneath the weight of their horses and armour. So many knights were drowned in the icy water that the remainder were forced to relinquish all their conquests, and for the time being the military power of the Teutonic Order was ignominiously swept away.

In Italy the cardinals did not elect a new pope until June 1243 and when they did they chose a Genoese jurist, Sinibaldo Fieschi, who took the name Innocent IV. He was inevitably a friend and supporter of the emperor, yet within eighteen months of his accession his own security was as uncertain as the survival of Christendom. Nobody knew why the Tartars had suddenly abandoned the destruction of defenceless Europe, but nobody doubted that they would return to complete it equally suddenly. In the summer after his election Innocent learned that the French crusade sent east by King Louis had been defeated by the soldiers of Jalal ad-Din, fighting on behalf of the Sultan of Egypt, and Jerusalem was again in Moslem hands. By the end of the same summer the papacy and the Holy Roman Empire were at war again. Innocent had been prepared to make almost any compromise to achieve peace with his friend, but he would not abandon the people of Lombardy to Frederick's rule, and once more the emperor resorted to force of arms. With Rome surrounded by imperial soldiers, the pope escaped in disguise and set up court at Lyons under the protection of King Louis.

From Lyons Innocent summoned the Thirteenth Ecumenical Council to assemble in June 1245. Of the three objectives which he was to lay before it, the most important from his own point of view was the deposition of the emperor, yet he was also prepared to dissipate such military strength as might be placed at his disposal by including on the agenda the organization of another crusade to the Holy Land. Before the council met he also made the first steps towards the fulfilment of his third objective, which was 'to seek a remedy against the Tartars'. From the Patriarch of Aquileia and a fugitive Russian bishop called Peter, the only men in Lyons who had first-hand experience of the invaders, he learned that the Tartars respected ambassadors, and so he decided to explore their mysterious empire and open negotiations by sending Dominican and Franciscan friars as his representatives. For some time these two missionary orders had provided the Church with its most successful diplomats, since their friars were not only scholars who could represent it at court, but also simple monks who could move among the common people and make their own political reports. At first he chose two Dominicans, Ascelinus of Lombardy and Andrew of Longjumeau, and two English Franciscans, John of Stanford and Abraham of Larde, but the two Englishmen were later replaced by two other Franciscans, Lawrence of Portugal and an Italian who spoke some of the eastern European languages, John of Plano Carpini. Each had two letters, one addressed to the King and nation of Tartars, outlining the doctrines of the Christian faith and exhorting them to embrace it, and another addressed to the King of the Tartars alone, deploring the cruelty and destruction of the recent campaign and calling for peace. The two Dominicans and Lawrence of Portugal were ordered to travel through the Middle East, deliver their letters to the first Mongol commander they met and then return to Lyons with as much information as they could gather. John of Plano Carpini was to travel through Russia and deliver his letter in person to the 'King of the Tartars'.

Friar John was the most experienced and distinguished of the ambassadors. Aged about sixty, he had been born in Plano Carpini, a town near Perugia now known as Magione, and had been one of Saint Francis's first disciples. He was a jovial monk whose loyalty and solicitude for his brethren had earned him their love and respect and whose charm and judgement had won him the friendship of the Bohemian and Silesian royal families. He was so heavily built and overweight that while he had been provincial vicar of Saxony he had found it easier to forsake the dignity of a horse and travel through the countryside on the back of a donkey, but although this might have made his journey through Russia more onerous, he was otherwise ideally suited for the mission. He was a discreet negotiator and a receptive and shrewd observer, and since it was unlikely that the 'King of the tartars' would make peace with a defenceless enemy or accept the Christian faith, his real objectives were to discover the extent of the Mongols' power, to observe the methods of their army and to persuade the schismatic Russian bishops and their princes to rejoin the Catholic church and accept the dominion of the Holy See in return for military assistance.

On Easter Sunday 1245 Friar John of Plano Carpini, accompanied by Friar Stephen of Bohemia, left Lyons and travelled through northern Europe, where all the rulers of the threatened kingdoms eagerly offered their support. In Bohemia Friar John's old friend Wenceslas welcomed them and sent them on to Breslau with an escort of Bohemian cavalry. Silesia had been inherited from Henry the Pious by his son Boleslaw II and in his citadel at Breslau, which had survived the Mongol campaign, the papal ambassadors met another Franciscan, Benedict the Pole, who had been campaigning with missionary zeal to bring about a reconciliation between the Russian church and the church of Rome. Explaining that this was also one of the purposes of his mission, Friar John persuaded him to join the embassy. Not only was his knowledge of eastern European languages greater than Friar John's, but also he had a stronger resolve than Friar Stephen, who from the outset had been terrified by the danger of the mission and even before reaching his native Bohemia had shown such signs of sickness that it had seemed as though Friar John might have to finish the journey alone. On reaching the new city that was emerging from the ruins of Cracow the ambassadors met Conrad of Mazovia who had ruled there after the war until his nephew Boleslaw the Chaste had returned and been reinstated by the citizens, and they found, 'by God's special grace', that Vasilko of Volynia was among the guests at court. From this Russian prince they learned how to treat with the Tartars. Vasilko and his brother Daniel of Galicia had already sent ambassadors to Batu offering the submission of their domains, and when the ambassadors had returned, Daniel had set out for Batu's camp to offer his allegiance in person and Vasilko had gone to Cracow to persuade the Poles to keep their soldiers out of Russia. Vasilko warned that ambassadors would be ignored unless they brought rich gifts as a mark of their respect and, 'not wishing that the affairs of the Lord Pope and the Church should be obstructed on this account', the monks spent most of the money that had been given to them by Wenceslas and Boleslaw on beaver furs. However, their purses were filled again by Duke Conrad and their stock of furs was multiplied by the generosity of his courtiers.

When the ambassadors set out for Russia Vasilko escorted them, attracted by their proposal of unity between the Russian Orthodox and the Roman Catholic churches. This would protect the western Russian principalities not only from the invading armies of Catholic Hungary and Poland, to which they had been regular victims before the Mongol invasion, but also from the ambitious crusades of the Teutonic Knights, and if the pope and the emperor were to settle their differences, it might even provide an alliance that would drive out their new Mongol masters. As soon as they reached Volynia, Vasilko assembled his barons and bishops and Friar John's proposals were accepted in principle, although the barons were afraid to make a final decision until Daniel returned from Batu's camp. Satisfied for the moment that their mission had succeeded as far as possible, the friars left for Kiev at the beginning of 1246.

With one of Vasilko's servants to guide them, their road lay through a desolate and frozen waste land. Most of the villages had been destroyed during the Mongol invasion and there was no food and little shelter. In spite of his bulk, the intense cold made Friar John so weak that he had to be carried through the snow in a cart and the fear of death that overcame him was not only due to the risk of exposure. The little party had to travel stealthily, hiding its camps by night and keeping the fires low, since all the young men in the area had been killed or carried off into slavery by the Mongols, leaving the old men, women and children in the few surviving villages and the travellers on the roads to become defenceless prey for roaming gangs of Lithuanian bandits.

Only when they reached the ruins of Kiev, which was garrisoned by a Mongol *minghan*, did the exhausted and apprehensive ambassadors come under the direct and arrogantly efficient protection of the Mongol Empire. From there on they were to be bullied and frightened and not always treated with the respect which they believed their office merited, but they could not complain that they were not supervised and protected. When they had rested, the *noyan* who commanded Kiev provided them with guides and, realizing that their European horses would not survive in the steppes in winter, gave them Mongol horses which had been trained to dig for grass beneath the snow. As the papal ambassadors were accustomed to the generous charity of princes and the dutiful assistance of their officers, he then found it necessary to point out to, them that his co-operation entitled him to some of their furs.

At the beginning of February, 'on the second day after the feast of the Purification of Our Lady', the three monks left Kiev and rode south towards the camp on the mouth of the Dnieper from which Batu's nephew Khurumsi controlled the western marches of his empire. In spite of the rest in Kiev, Friar Stephen was still sick and as the journey progressed, his terror of the Mongols increased until he became so weak and frightened that he was unfit to travel. In each town that they passed through the Mongol governor gave them fresh horses, but at one town, where the governor was an Alan rogue called Micheas who had sent a messenger to Kiev saying that he had been instructed to lead them to Khurumsi, they found that he had only sent for them so that he could have his own share of their bounty, and they were not allowed to continue their journey until he had helped himself to their furs.

On 'the first Friday after Ash Wednesday' the friars were sighted by a patrol from a Mongol camp and as they were preparing to rest for the night the soldiers burst in on them demanding to know who they were. The Mongol soldiers must have found it difficult to believe that these simple holy men were the ambassadors of a great lord; although they accepted their explanation and galloped back to their camp, next morning, when the friars set out again, the camp commanders were waiting on the road to interview them. Once the officers understood the importance of their mission they sent a messenger ahead to announce their arrival and even dismounted and gave them some of their own horses as extra pack animals. Naturally this kindness further depleted the friars' supply of furs, but the officers also agreed to look after the terrified Friar Stephen and escort him back to Kiev when he was stronger.

At Khurumsi's camp Friar John and Friar Benedict were made to pitch their tents outside its perimeter and were not granted an audience until Khurumsi had been given more of their furs than they could afford. When at last he sent for them they had their first experience of Mongol ceremony. They knelt three times at the entrance to his tent and were warned not to insult him by putting their feet on the wooden threshold, and when they entered they explained their purpose on bended knee. Khurumsi wanted to have their letters read to him, but he could not find anyone in his camp who could read Latin and nor could the interpreter who had been given to the friars by the commander of Kiev, so he sent them on their way, escorted by two of his *arban* commanders and one of Batu's *noyans*.

The two friars with their escort and attendants set out for Sarai on 26 February. Always riding at a trot, they changed horses three or four times a day and sometimes rode through the night, yet it took them over five weeks to cover the six hundred and fifty miles from the Dnieper to the Volga. As Friar John described it, they set out for Batu's camp on the Monday after the first Sunday of Quadragesima and it was not before the Wednesday in Holy Week that they reached it. In spite of the hardships of the journey the friars observed the Lenten fast, eating nothing but millet with salt and water, until they became so feeble that they could hardly ride. Nevertheless Friar John continued to record everything that he learned, particularly the disposition of Batu's soldiers.

The armies of the Golden Horde were deployed along the four rivers of its empire; beyond the Dnieper in the west stood the army of Khurumsi, which was probably no more than two *tumens*, although Friar John recorded its strength at sixty thousand men; between the Dnieper and the Don stood three *tumens* under Mauci; to the east of the Don, Batu's brother-in-law Katan commanded two *tumens*; and the main army of three or four *tumens*

under Batu himself controlled the Volga from Sarai. It was significant of Batu's misgivings about the court at Karakorum that the
eastern boundary of his empire was also guarded by two *tumens*
which patrolled the banks of the river Ural.

Since his withdrawal from Hungary, Batu had been consolidating his empire. One by one the Russian princes had offered him
their allegiance, but although his rule extended into Bulgaria and
as far north as Novgorod, he did not exercise military control
beyond Kiev.

The first prince to offer his allegiance in person was Yaroslav of
Novgorod, who arrived in Sarai in 1242, shortly after Batu's return.
In name at least, Yaroslav had become Grand Duke of Vladimir and
Suzdal, after his brother Yuri had been killed with the rest of his
family during the invasion. When Batu appointed him to rule all
these territories as a vassal prince of the Mongol Empire, he sent his
son Constantine to Mongolia to pledge his allegiance to the regent.

Meanwhile in the south-west of Russia, the Princes of Chernigov
and Galicia had been perpetuating their weakness by maintaining
the animosity that had existed before the Mongol invasion. But in
1245 Prince Michael of Chernigov's army, led by his son Rostislav
and supported by Poles and Hungarians, was routed by Daniel of
Galicia and Vasilko of Volynia. It was as a result of this victory that
Vasilko went to Cracow to make terms with the Poles; and Daniel
went to Sarai to offer his allegiance in person, because his victory
over another vassal prince had made him potentially powerful and
Batu was threatening to put Galicia under the rule of a military
governor. At Sarai Daniel was diplomatically respectful and humble
and Batu liked him. At a banquet Batu asked if he drank *kumiz* like
the Mongols and Daniel answered: 'Until now I did not, but now I
do as you command and I drink it.' To which Batu replied: 'You
are now one of ours,' and since he was more used to it ordered that
Daniel be given a goblet of wine. A Galician chronicler was
appalled to record that his great prince knelt and called himself the
khan's slave, but Daniel knew that it was in his own interest to
exploit Batu's good will and when he returned to Galicia he
demonstrated his allegiance to the world by re-equipping his
soldiers with Mongol uniforms and weapons.

The khan's good will was not shared by the Princes of Chernigov.
Andrew, the son of Mstislav, who had been killed at the battle of
Kalka, was executed for no more than exporting horses without a

licence, and when Prince Michael came to offer his allegiance after Daniel, he was treated like an enemy. Batu did not trust a vassal prince who had attacked a neighbour and imported foreign soldiers into his empire. Prince Michael, accompanied by a mischievous *boyar* who encouraged him to defy the khan, was made to walk between two fires, a superstitious ceremony which was supposed to remove all evil intent, but he refused to kneel before a statue of Chingis Khan and since this could be interpreted as a refusal to submit, Batu was delighted to be given cause to order his execution.

At Karakorum, Mangku, with Batu's support, had done everything that he could to oppose the election of Kuyuk, but Toregene had been ruthless. After the death of her strongest ally Chagatai in 1242, she had systematically replaced all the powerful officials in the empire with Kuyuk's supporters. The governor of eastern Persia was executed and Yalavach, the governor of Transoxiana, fled to Batu's camp at Sarai. Yeh-Lu Ch'u-Ts'ai, the most respected servant of the empire, was replaced as chancellor by Abd al-Rahman who had persuaded Toregene that he could double her income in taxes from northern China. Broken-hearted, the former chancellor died in 1244 at the age of fifty-five. He was taken away and buried at the foot of Wan Shen mountain, nine miles outside Peking, and in the eighteenth century a temple was built over the tomb which contains statues of the mandarin and his wife. After his death, suspecting that a man who had controlled the finances of the empire for so long must have amassed a great fortune, Toregene's guards broke into his house, but all they found were collections of inscribed stones, maps, manuscripts and musical instruments. With Toregene's political power unassailable, Mangku and Batu could do no more than delay the inevitable election of Kuyuk, and by the time Friar John and Friar Benedict reached Sarai, Karakorum was preparing for the official ceremony.

On their arrival the friars, like all foreigners, were made to camp a league beyond the other tents. Some of Batu's officers who came out to ask what gifts they had brought for him were disdainful when they saw the few remaining bundles of beaver furs, which the friars explained had been bought with their own money since their lord pope did not send rich presents, but Batu had been informed of their mission by the *yam* messengers from Khurumsi, and when he had readily accepted their humble tribute they were summoned to his tent on Good Friday.

At first the frightened friars refused to pass between two fires, but they did so when they were reassured by the officers that it was only a ritual, and they were then searched for weapons. After kneeling three times at the entrance, the friars stepped over the threshold, knelt before Batu Khan and gave him the letters from the pope. Batu sat on a raised platform with one of his wives beside him and the rest of his family sat in front on a low bench in the middle of the tent. Behind them on the floor, which was covered with fine carpets, sat the courtiers and officers with the men on the right and the women on the left. Near the door stood a large table bearing food and drink in gold and silver vases. Unlike the *yurts* of his soldiers, Batu's tents were made of linen; as Friar John wrote, 'They are large and quite handsome, and used to belong to the King of Hungary.' Interpreters were summoned and while the letters were being translated the friars were told to sit on the left with the women. Since a commander's tent, like the rest of the camp, faced south, the left was the east and the position of honour. On their way to the supreme khan at Karakorum, ambassadors always sat on the side of the rising sun, but once they had been granted an audience and were returning to their master, they sat on the side of the sunset. No one who spoke Mongol could also read Latin and so the letters had first to be translated into Russian and then into Persian. Batu's father and grandfather had been illiterate, but Friar John recorded that when he was given the Mongol versions of the letters he read them through carefully himself. When he had finished, he said nothing and the friars were ordered to return to their tents.

Next day they were summoned back and met at the door by one of the officers. Batu had commanded that some of their attendants were to remain in his camp and to rest before returning to Lyons, since he expected that they would want to report to the pope, but the two friars were to leave at once for Karakorum. Their letters were not addressed to Batu, but to 'the King of the Tartars', and although he had not yet been inaugurated, if they hurried they might be in time for the ceremony.

Two days later, fearful that they might never return, Friar John and Friar Benedict said mass and with only a few servants and the two soldiers who had been given to them as an escort by Khurumsi set out weeping on the journey of nearly three thousand miles to Karakorum. Their other servants, to whom they had given letters for the pope, never reached Lyons. When they crossed the Don they were intercepted by Mauci and detained until the ambassadors returned.

Through wind-swept steppes, parched desert and frozen mountains, the friars travelled at a rate of over twenty-five miles a day, along the routes of the well-established *yam*, changing horses and resting by night in the staging posts and sometimes arriving so late that they did not eat until next morning. They rode along the north of the Aral Sea, through steppes which were still littered with the bones of defeated nomads, and past ruined towns on the banks of the Syr Darya to Otrar. From there they travelled through Kara Khitai, resting for the day at the new Mongol city of Omyl at Tacheng, where the governor gave a banquet for them at which they first encountered the Mongols' custom of clapping their hands when their guests drank, and then on through the lands of the Naimans in western Mongolia towards Karakorum. Friar John wrote,

The weather there is astonishingly irregular, for in the middle of summer, when other places are enjoying very great heat, there is fierce thunder and lightning which causes the death of many men, and at the same time there are very heavy falls of snow. There are also hurricanes of bitterly cold winds, so violent that at times men can ride on horseback only with great effort. When we were before the ordu – that is what the camps of the emperor and chief men are called – we lay prostrate on account of the force of the wind and we could scarcely see owing to the great clouds of dust.

The journey took nearly fifteen weeks. It began at Sarai on 8 April, 'the day of the Resurrection of Our Lord', and ended on 22 July, 'the Feast of the Blessed Mary Magdalen'. But the ambassadors never saw the Mongol capital. They halted a few miles west of it at the splendid camp which had been built to house four thousand ambassadors and the retinues of all the Mongol lords and foreign princes who had assembled to witness the enthronement of a new supreme khan.

Outside the bustling camp, Mongol commanders paraded their soldiers in ceremonial uniforms which were changed every day and the friars were greatly impressed by the harness and breastplates of the officers' horses which were decorated with 'about twenty marks' worth of gold'. Inside, lords and princes banqueted and discussed the imminent election, but the result was never in doubt:

whenever Kuyuk emerged from a tent he was greeted by the soldiers with singing.

The friars were supplied with food and given a *yurt* with soldiers to guard it and after a few days' rest they were formally received in the great tent that stood in the centre of the camp where Toregene held court. Around her were all the princes of the imperial family except Batu, who had broken a sacred tradition by failing to attend the election. Her tent had two entrances, one of which was as yet unguarded and reserved for the new khan, and it was surrounded by a stockade where the excited crowds were kept at bay by soldiers armed with clubs and untipped arrows. When they appeared before her, the regent honoured the pope's ambassadors by offering them a drink and after they had observed the proprieties by accepting the cup of mead, the embarrassed friars found themselves subjected to the good-humoured encouragements of her courtiers who tried to make them drunk.

The rest of the time that led up to the ceremony the friars spent with the other ambassadors and princes who assembled each day with the Mongol *noyans* outside the great tent. Among them were princes from every nation in the empire and from many beyond its borders, yet when they dined, the places of honour were always given to the ambassadors of the pope and Grand Duke Yaroslav of Vladimir and Suzdal, the accredited representative of Batu Khan.

The election and the enthronement were held in a valley a few miles from the camp, in a huge yellow tent lined with brocade and supported by gold-plated pillars. The ceremony was postponed by hailstorms until 24 August, but on that day, as had been expected, Kuyuk Khan ascended a bejewelled throne while all the Mongol *noyans*, foreign princes and ambassadors, except the friars who ungraciously refused to humble themselves since they were not Mongol subjects, knelt before him in submission. The coronation was followed by several days of extravagant feasting and dancing and as soon as the celebrations came to an end, the foreign princes and ambassadors were formally received one by one in the yellow tent.

When the two friars took their turn, they were asked by the court officials what tribute they had brought. Outside the tent stood fifty camels with brocade-canopied saddles, beyond them were five hundred wagons filled with gold, silver and silken gowns and inside the tent there were so many silks, jewels and splendid furs 'that it was a marvel to see'. All the friars' beaver furs had been used up on their journey and they were the only envoys who brought nothing. It was to be over two months before the responsibilities of his new office would allow Kuyuk the time to deal with the letters from the pope, but he expressed his displeasure at the lack of tribute by ordering that his hospitality to the friars should be limited, and since the markets were too far away, they would have starved if they had not been fed by a Russian goldsmith called Cosmas who had made the imperial throne and seal.

To the surprise of his opponents, the administration of the hedonistic new emperor was neither as self-indulgent nor as corrupt as his mother's had been and many of the worst decisions and appointments of her reign were reversed: Abd al-Rahman was tried and executed for extortion and replaced by Yalavach; Chinkai, who had been second in Ogedei's council to Yeh-Lu Ch'u-Ts'ai, was restored to office; Baiju, who had been given command of the armies in Persia, was replaced by Eljigidei; the aunt who had been suspected of murdering the khan's father was executed; and Fatima was found guilty of sorcery, sewn up in a sack and thrown into a river.

The khan's mother may well have been embittered by this ingratitude, but it was more probably her resentment at Batu's opposition and his failure to attend the election that caused her to continue her treacherous interference in the affairs of the empire. She invited Batu's representative, Grand Duke Yaroslav, to dine with her and offered him food with her own hands 'as if to honour him'. That night, when he returned to his *yurt* he became sick and when within a week he was dead, the dowager empress sent secret messengers to Alexander Nevsky inviting him to come to Karakorum and be confirmed as his father's heir.

It was not until the beginning of November that the friars were granted the first of several audiences with the khan. Although he had already received translations of their letters from Batu, they were made to write down everything that they intended to say so that Kuyuk and his council would be briefed before the audience. They found him shrewd and serious and from the many Nestorian Christian clerks at his court they learned that he was always solemn and had never been seen to smile, a public image which was particularly to his credit since his private life was as dedicated to wine and women as his father's had been. It was these Christians who assured the delighted friars that Kuyuk preferred their religion to all others and always had the Christian chapel placed in front of his tent; it was the religion of his mother and they were convinced that it would not be long before he was ready to receive baptism himself.

Kuyuk's partiality, however, was not evidenced by his reaction to the letters from the pope. Having seen Europe for himself, he was no more awed by the leader of its church than he had been by the commanders of its armies, and since one of his own titles was 'the Son of Heaven', he scorned the solicitations of a man who also claimed to speak for God and answered his rebukes with threats. In his curt letter of reply, he alleged that he did not understand why the pope had asked him to be baptized, nor why he should have found it strange that his armies had conquered the Hungarians and other Christians since they had murdered Mongol ambassadors and refused to accept the dominion of an empire that had been ordained by God. Pointing out that the pope should know better than any man that no one could rule all the empires from sunrise to sunset unless it were through the will of God, he warned that if the pope and all the kings of Christendom did not accept God's will and come to Karakorum to pay homage, he would know them to be his enemies.

With the help of a Russian knight, who had been in Grand Duke Yaroslav's retinue, the friars translated the Mongol letter into Latin, and Chinkai, who had questioned every word as they wrote it, gave them a Persian version against which it could be checked if the pope should ever find anyone who could read Persian. When the letter had been translated, the last interview was at an end and the friars returned to their *yurt* with the soldiers who had been delegated to escort them back to Russia. One of these soldiers suggested that they should ask for another audience since the khan was anxious to send his own ambassadors to the pope and the conventions of his court required that the invitation should come from them. But Friar John declined: he feared for their safety, 'since our people are for the most part arrogant and hasty', and above all he feared 'that they would see the dissensions and wars among us and that it would encourage them to march against us'.

On 13 November 1246, 'the Feast of Saint Brice', they were given permission to leave and after saying farewell to the dowager empress, who gave them each a fox fur gown with quilted lining, they set out on the long journey home. They knew that Kuyuk was preparing for war again and that they brought little comfort for the people of eastern Europe, but they did not know that the letter which they carried was not so ominous as the virtual declarations of war that had been given to the ambassadors of the Master of the Assassins and the Caliph of Baghdad.

Since the death of Ogedei, the Mongol Empire had continued to expand in Persia through the campaigns of Baiju: Georgia had become a Mongol domain and Kuyuk had divided it between the son of Queen Rusudan and the bastard son of George IV; after his defeat in battle, the Sultan of Rum, in whose army crusaders had fought as mercenaries, had paid tribute and attended the election to swear allegiance; and the Christian King of Little Armenia, Hayton I, had sensibly volunteered to become a vassal prince of the Mongol khan. The Mongol Empire was now so powerful that for the grandson of Chingis Khan the dominion of the world was an achievable ambition and the only potential obstacle was not a powerful enemy but his own cousin, the independent khan of the Golden Horde. Batu had sent his ambassador to swear allegiance and since the election he had shown no antagonism, even when that ambassador had been murdered, but Kuyuk did not trust him and for the time being he made no plans for a return to Europe. Instead he assembled a new army in Mongolia and sent it southeast under Subedei to complete the conquest of the Sung and ordered Eljigidei to conscript additional *tumens* from Georgia and Armenia and prepare to advance into Syria.

The friars travelled through Kara Khitai with the ambassador of the Sultan of Egypt, and, slowed down by a bitter winter, they did not reach Sarai until the 'Day of the Ascension of Our Lord', six months after their departure from Kuyuk's camp. From there they rode across Russia, calling on Mauci to collect their servants on 'the Saturday after the Octave of Pentecost', and on 9 June 1247, 'fifteen days before the feast of Saint John the Baptist', they were greeted at Kiev as though they had 'risen from the dead'.

In Galicia the friars stayed for eight days with Daniel and Vasilko, who had received another ambassador from the pope during their absence, and in return for papal recognition and the promise of a Christian army from western Europe, the princes agreed 'to have the Lord Pope for their particular lord and father and the Holy Roman Church as their lady and mistress'. When the decision had been endorsed by a council of barons and bishops, a

gratified Friar John and an exultant Friar Benedict set out eagerly
for Lyons with Daniel's ambassadors.

They travelled through Poland and Hungary, pausing briefly to
report all that they had seen and learned to King Bela, who since
their departure had been struggling valiantly to restore his kingdom. His success in reclaiming his western *departments*, however,
had only served to weaken the military power of the rest of Europe:
after crossing the river Leitha on 15 June 1246 he had destroyed
the army of Austria and killed its contentious duke.

On 18 November 1247 the friars arrived at Lyons, two years and
seven months after Friar John had left it and just over a year after
they had set out from Kuyuk's camp. With the letters and ambassadors from Daniel of Galicia, Friar John was able to report the
success of his mission in Russia, but from the Mongol court he
brought nothing but threats. 'It is their intention to overthrow the
whole world and reduce it to slavery', he warned, and he advocated
that the rulers of Christendom should unite and march against
them before they began to spread their rule again. He held out
some hope of a respite because of the estrangement between Kuyuk
and Batu, and, although he did not believe that the khan intended
to be baptized, his news that there were many Nestorian Christians
in positions of authority at the Mongol court was a consolation to
the pope. A few months earlier, after delivering his letters near
Tabriz to the commander of the first Mongol patrol that he met,
Andrew of Longjumeau had returned with a letter from Simeon,
the Patriarch of the Nestorian Christians, recognizing the pope as
his lord and master. Apart from this allegiance, however, Friar
Andrew's mission had achieved more harm than good. It had
aroused the suspicions of the Sultan of Egypt, who believed that the
pope was attempting to enlist Mongol support in the war against
the Holy Roman Emperor, and the Moslem rulers began to fear that
if the emperor should be defeated, the suspected alliance might
turn its attentions to Islam.

Both Friar John and Friar Benedict wrote records of their
journey. The longest and most detailed was Friar John's which
contained an analysis of the methods of the Mongol army, as well
as some naïve suggestions as to how they should be countered. He
carried it with him so that it could be read aloud in the monasteries
he visited and since there were so many sceptics who tried to discredit it, he added paragraphs which gave further details about the

places he had visited and named the Venetian and Genoese merchants whom he had met there. Although Friar John's account of everything he had seen was accurate and objective, like so many scholars of his age he was prepared to believe and record many of the legendary phenomena that he had not seen. In his chapter on the history of the Mongols, for example, he described a land where 'every female had a human form and every male had the shape of a dog', and added that the existence of these monsters had been confirmed by the Russian clerks at the Mongol court. Nevertheless his record, together with that of Friar Benedict, provided a great deal of new and historically invaluable information. Above all, they were the records of the first western Europeans to make the formidable journey into the heart of mysterious Asia. It was not until seven years after their return that a boy whose epic memoirs were to eclipse Friar John's was born in Venice and christened in honour of his rich uncle who owned a warehouse in the Mongol protectorate at Soldaia, Marco Polo.

The 'dissensions and wars' which Friar John left behind had grown fiercer in his absence; the fighting between the supporters of the pope and the emperor had spread from Italy to Germany, and within a few months of his return Friar John was again entrusted with the responsibilities of a papal ambassador. He was sent to the court of King Louis to persuade him to abandon the crusade that he had been planning for three years and lead his army into Italy instead to fight against the emperor, but the devout king would not forswear his vow and on 24 August 1248 he and his queen set sail for Cyprus with Andrew of Longjumeau among their retinue.

On 17 September the French crusaders landed at Limassol. Soon after, Louis met some Armenians who had been sent to the King of Cyprus by the Armenian king's brother with a letter describing the growth of Christian influence at the Mongol court and suggesting that the entire empire might be converted. Then, on 20 December in Nicosia, to his astonishment and delight, he received two ambassadors from the camp of Eljigidei. They were Nestorian Christians called David and Mark, one of whom had met Friar Andrew during his travels in Georgia, and they carried a letter in which the Mongol commander, who claimed that he had been charged by his khan to protect all Christians in western Asia and rebuild their churches, declared that he prayed to God for the success of the French crusade. This assurance of Mongol good will was surprising enough, but the letter also asked the French king to listen to the words which the ambassadors had been told to say to him, and when they had pleased him further by announcing that the Mongol khan had been baptized as a Christian and that Eljigidei had followed his example, the Nestorians delivered the message which their commander had not dared to put in writing. Eljigidei intended to march against Baghdad at the end of the winter and if the King of France were to coincide his landing in Egypt with that attack, the two most powerful rulers in Islam would be unable to come to each other's assistance and the victorious armies of France and the Mongol Empire would advance on two fronts to liberate the Holy Land.

Among the aspects of the Mongol armies which Friar John had failed to emphasize was the efficiency of their intelligence. They had known that King Louis was planning a crusade and Ascelinus of Lombardy, who had reached Baiju's camp at the same time as Eljigidei arrived to take over command, had been interrogated about it before being sent home with a letter which was identical to Friar John's. The story of Kuyuk's baptism was almost certainly true since it is recorded by the Moslem historian Juvaini, but it is more likely to have been motivated by self-interest than by profound conviction, and the alliance of the French crusaders with the newly-Christian khan was far more to the advantage of the Mongol Empire than Christendom. Neither Kuyuk nor Eljigidei believed that King Louis was capable of defeating the Sultan of Egypt, but at least he could keep him busy while their armies attacked Baghdad. Nevertheless the ingenuous King of France was overjoyed and it looked as though the Egyptian sultan's worst fears were about to be realized.

At once King Louis informed the pope and prepared an embassy to the Mongol khan which was entrusted to Andrew of Longjumeau. On 27 January 1249 Andrew, with a few other friars and the two Mongol ambassadors, set sail for Antioch carrying a portable chapel and a fragment of the True Cross for Kuyuk, and an oral message for Eljigidei that King Louis would comply with his plans.

In the spring, while King Louis was landing in Egypt as promised, the friars reached the camp of Eljigidei, which was near Tabriz: the Mongol commander had not advanced against Baghdad. During the absence of his Nestorian ambassadors the balance of power had shifted in the imperial family. In 1248 Kuyuk had summoned Batu to meet him in the Ili valley, which lay between their domains, so that he might swear his allegiance in person and the breach between them might be healed. After obediently setting out, Batu halted near Alakmak on receipt of a secret message from Mangku's mother Sorkaktani, warning him that Kuyuk intended to have him arrested and executed. By then, however, the danger was over: while he too was travelling towards the appointed valley, Kuyuk Khan had died of drink at the age of forty-two. Kuyuk's widow Oghul-Ghaimish was now the official regent and, like Toregene, she was attempting to rig the election in favour of her nephew Siremun, but her only allies were the descendants of Ogedei and Chagatai. Tolui's widow Sorkaktani had set herself up in opposition and with the support of most of the *noyans* and the other princes, particularly Batu, who as senior prince of the empire had refused the throne for himself, she was campaigning in favour of her own son Mangku. Eljigidei, who owed his appointment to Kuyuk, had therefore postponed his campaign until the election was settled and since he did not dare to answer the ambassadors himself, he sent them on to Oghul-Ghaimish, who had abandoned Karakorum and set up her camp in Tarbagatai.

When Andrew and the other friars reached her at the beginning of 1250, the regent saw them only as an opportunity to increase her own prestige. She accepted the gifts that had been sent to her husband as though they were tribute, but she ignored the offer of an alliance. Since the word 'Frank' was used in the east to describe all the peoples of Europe, she announced that these were the ambassadors of the European kings who had come to swear their allegiance to her, and after publicly presenting them with letters which demanded that Louis should come to pay homage in person and threatened an invasion if he did not, she sent them home with her own ambassadors, who would ensure that they did not try to visit Batu or Mangku.

The stratagem did nothing to promote her nephew's cause. At Alakmak Batu had summoned an election council, but the princes of the houses of Ogedei and Chagatai had refused to attend because an election could only be held in Mongolia itself, and when they also boycotted the council which was assembled in the Mongolian steppe under Batu's brother Berke, they were presented with a *fait accompli*. On 1 July 1251 Mangku was elected supreme khan. Some of the descendants of Ogedei, including Kadan, who had served with Mangku in the European campaign, accepted the election and swore allegiance, but a few of the thwarted princes, together with those councillors who feared for the loss of their office, resorted to intrigue. They planned that Siremun and Buri would go to Mangku's camp with armed escorts, hundreds of servants and concealed weapons in their baggage train, pretending that they had come to pay tribute, and once they were in his presence they would arrest him with the approval of the councillors and declare the election invalid. But their plot was discovered. While searching the steppe for a strayed mule, one of Mangku's soldiers noticed the weapons in the princes' wagons. When they arrived, their soldiers and servants were dismissed outside the camp and, after they had been allowed to join in the celebration of Mangku's election, it was the conspirators who were arrested. Investigations and trials followed. Chinkai was executed; Oghul-Ghaimish suffered the same fate as Fatima; Chagatai's grandson Buri was sentenced and handed over to the vengeful Batu for execution; and through the intercession of Mangku's brother Kubilai, Siremun was spared and sent to serve in the army in China, where he was later killed on Mangku's orders. Among the seventy *noyans* who also died for their complicity were the sons of Eljigidei, who were horribly put to death by being made to swallow stones until they choked, and even their innocent father was arrested and executed by Batu.

Friar Andrew rejoined King Louis at the village of Caesarea, near Acre, in the narrow strip of states along the Palestinian coast that was the crusaders' last foothold in Islam. The friar's report was exasperating and the king believed that the Mongols had tricked him into a token submission, but the abuse of his ambassadors was nothing to the humiliation that he had suffered himself. The crusade in Egypt had been a disaster.

On 5 June 1249 Louis landed on the west bank of the Nile, took Damietta unopposed and then advanced towards Cairo, but his vanguard was destroyed by a rising young Mamluk commander called Baybars and after a briefly effective retreat the starving French army was forced to surrender. The king, half dead with dysentery, was led away in chains. In the days that followed Christian prisoners were mercilessly slaughtered and when the king eventually purchased his freedom for a million gold *bezants* and set out for Acre on 7 May 1250, out of sixty thousand men only twelve thousand had survived to sail with him.

During the campaign the Sultan of Egypt had died, but a beautiful and devoted wife, Shajar al-Durr (Spray of Pearls), had kept his death secret, issuing orders to the commanders as though they had been given to her by her husband. After the French surrender the news was revealed and the sultan's drunken and cowardly son returned from exile to inherit his empire, but the Mamluks mutinied and a few days before the French survivors set sail for Acre, they murdered the sultan's heir. Against the horrified but ineffective opposition of the Caliph of Baghdad, who mocked the Egyptians for allowing themselves to be governed by a woman, Shajar al-Durr was proclaimed sultana, and when she married Aybak, the commander-in-chief of the Mamluks, the vassal princes of Syria, who refused to be ruled by anyone who was not descended from Saladin, let alone a woman or a former slave, crowned al-Nasir, the King of Aleppo, as their independent sultan. Fate had been even more cruel to King Louis than he realized: by the time Friar Andrew returned from Mongolia the last unconquered Moslem princes, like the rulers of Europe, were divided by intrigue and war, and during the four years that the French king remained in Acre, the Mongol armies were preparing for the greatest military offensive that Islam had ever faced.

Once his throne had been secured by the purge, Mangku gave orders that the campaigns which had been planned under Kuyuk were to be continued on an even greater scale. A census was ordered in the outlying areas of the empire so that the size of his armies could be increased still further, and since the new empires that these armies would conquer and control were to be governed by members of his own family, command was to be given, not to the *orloks*, but to the imperial princes themselves. While Batu would be left free to act as he chose in the west, Mangku and his brother Kubilai would extend the empire in the east and his brother Hulegu would advance through Syria towards the borders of Egypt, to create a new empire in the heart of Islam. If Mangku had known about King Louis' offer of an alliance he might have made use of it, but now that the khans of Karakorum and Sarai were united, he did not need it, and through the interference of Oghul-Ghaimish the crusading kings of western Europe had lost the opportunity to share in the liberation of Jerusalem.

Mangku's gratitude to the cousin who had given him the imperial throne had made Batu an independent emperor and it was to him and not the new khan at Karakorum that the Russian princes renewed their allegiance. Daniel of Galicia and Vasilko of Volynia had already made their submission to Batu, but the two other influential princes were technically the vassals of the supreme khan. After the murder of their father, the Grand Duke Yaroslav, Alexander Nevsky and his brother Andrew had been summoned to Karakorum, where Kuyuk had confirmed Andrew as the new Grand Duke of Vladimir and Suzdal and Alexander had been appointed Prince of Kiev. Kuyuk had given Alexander Kiev in the hope of creating a dependant of his own in the west of Batu's empire, but Kiev was under the direct control of Batu's soldiers and Alexander had preferred to remain in the unscathed and un-occupied domains of Novgorod. Unlike the other princes, Alexander's allegiance to the Mongols was genuine: he was too devoutly orthodox to abandon his faith for the sake of an army and whereas Galicia and Volynia, to whom Vladimir and Suzdal had been allied by the marriage of Grand Duke Andrew to the daughter of Prince Daniel, could expect willing assistance from the threat-ened Catholic kingdoms of Poland and Hungary, the only neigh-bours of Novgorod were the Teutonic Knights and the Swedes, against whose aggressive ambitions Mongol mastery was a powerful defence.

Alexander Nevsky was, therefore, the first to go to Sarai and offer his allegiance to Batu's Christian son Sartak, who had been given responsibility for the government of Russia. But his brother Andrew raised an army and refused to join him. If Andrew believed that his father-in-law was ready to support him, he mis-calculated; Daniel of Galicia continued his pretence of enthusiastic allegiance. Andrew's isolated army was destroyed by a punitive expedition from Sarai, the lands of Vladimir were laid waste again, and when Andrew fled to find refuge in Sweden, Alexander Nevsky was appointed Grand Duke of Vladimir in his place.

Daniel of Galicia was waiting for the papal army that had been promised by John of Plano Carpini, but his hopes, which had been briefly raised by the death of the Emperor Frederick in December 1250, were beginning to fade again. Although the pope had returned to Rome, the emperor's son Conrad had taken up his father's cause and was reversing some of the defeats that had been

suffered in Italy, and John of Plano Carpini, the most ardent advocate of an offensive in Russia, died in 1252. The pope had rewarded
Friar John with the archbishopric of Antivari in Dalmatia, but he
did not have the power to follow his advice and his only fulfilment
of the pledges that had been made to Daniel was an empty gesture.
In 1253 he sent an ambassador to Galicia who crowned Daniel in a
Catholic ceremony at Drogichin.

From that time on Daniel's dreams of a crusade against the
Mongols disappeared and only the fear of greater oppression
replaced them. Alexander Nevsky, the most powerful prince in
Russia, was now a loyal Mongol subject; Christendom remained as
divided as Islam had become; and across four thousand miles, from
the Black Sea to the Yellow Sea, all the nations were united and
preparing to march out of the heartland under the yak-tailed
standards of the mightiest empire the world had ever known.

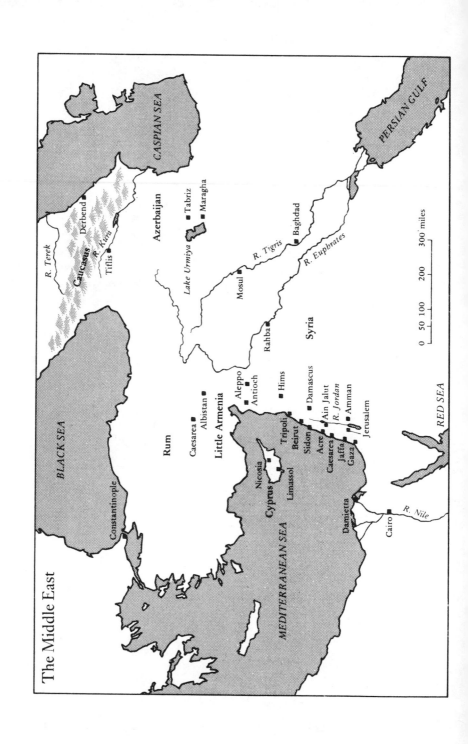

The Middle East

10
The Tartar Crusaders

THE crusaders in Acre received regular reports from the Nestorians and the Armenians, confirming the spread of Christianity in the Mongol Empire, and, although these reports were no consolation to the commanders who had been disillusioned by the failure of Friar Andrew's embassy, to one less sceptical missionary monk they were an inspiration. He was a young Flemish Franciscan called William of Rubruck, who had been deeply distressed by Friar Andrew's description of the suffering that he had seen among the Catholic German slaves in Buri's labour gangs, and soon after he learned that the new governor of Russia was a Christian, he determined to set out in search of these slaves, to bring them the consolation of their church and to test their masters' tolerance by preaching the Christian gospel among the Mongols. Naturally King Louis was reluctant to give the mission his blessing, lest the friar should be seen as another ambassador offering allegiance, but he was still anxious to discover the intentions of the Mongol armies in Syria, and, since Friar William was prepared to act as an unofficial observer, he eventually agreed to give him one letter addressed only to Sartak, from one Christian prince to another, requesting that the missionary be given safe conduct to preach their faith among his people.

At the beginning of 1253 Friar William set out from Acre with an Italian Franciscan, Bartholomew of Cremona, one of King Louis' secretaries called Gosset and a Syrian interpreter. They travelled via Constantinople and Soldaia, and on 31 July arrived at Sartak's camp between the Don and the Volga. They were courteously received, but Sartak, who expressed his respect for King Louis as 'the greatest Lord among the Franks', found it difficult to believe that they were not ambassadors or even spies. On the pretext that their letter was ambiguous and presented him with 'certain difficulties', he sent them on to Sarai to report to his father. 'When I saw Batu's *ordu*', wrote Friar William, 'I was overcome with fear, for his own houses seemed like a great city stretching out a long way and crowded round on every side by people to a distance of three or four leagues'. Batu, whom Friar William described unhelpfully as 'about the height of my lord Jean de Beaumont' and red in the face, was as courteous as Sartak but equally suspicious. After declaring that only the supreme khan himself could give them permission to preach their faith, he ordered that Gosset should be sent back to Sartak as a hostage and gave the two friars one of his officers to escort them to Mangku at Karakorum. On their journey they enquired about the German slaves, but learned that after Buri's execution his slaves had been sent to work the mines in the Tien Shan mountains, and they never found them. They did, however, meet many Christians, including a Cuman who had been converted by Franciscans in Hungary and spoke to them in Latin. Furthermore, in some of the camps and towns where they rested they were invited by the commanders to read prayers, which at first encouraged them to preach, until the incompetence of their interpreter drove them to abandon it.

Mangku was camped on the north-east of the Altai mountains, where the friars reached him shortly after Christmas, and on 4 January 1254 they were granted an audience in a tent lined with cloth of gold where Mangku sat on a couch with one of his wives, wearing a 'speckled and shiny fur like sealskin' and playing with his falcons. After the traditional Mongol hospitality the interview was unfortunately brief, since Friar William was afraid that the khan's judgement had been influenced by the wine and his own already inadequate interpreter was completely drunk. Through Mangku's Nestorian interpreter, however, he explained that he and Friar Bartholomew had brought neither gold nor silver and that they came only to ask his permission to remain in his lands and teach men the laws of God. Before granting their request, Mangku answered: 'Just as the sun sheds his rays everywhere, so my power and the power of Batu extends everywhere; we have no need of your gold or silver.'

For the next two months the friars remained in the khan's camp and were regularly interrogated by his ministers, who were never convinced that they were not ambassadors. Mangku was kind to them; he gave them fur coats and he asked the Armenian monk who presided over the chapel in the camp to take care of them, but since they asserted that they were not ambassadors they were denied the privileges of ambassadors and without the right to ask for an audience they were unable to speak to the khan unless he summoned them.

The Armenian monk, whose name was Sergius, had arrived in the camp only a month before the friars, after apparently receiving a vision in Jerusalem, in which God had commanded him to go to Mangku. Although they were appalled to discover that he had advised the khan to become a Christian so that the pope and the Franks would obey him, and as time passed they were shocked by his heresy, the friars respected him as though he were their bishop. It was not until he was travelling home again that Friar William learned that Sergius was merely a weaver who had set himself up as a visionary monk in order to gain influence at the Mongol court. Sergius maintained that the khan favoured the Christians and was contemplating baptism, but the friars could see for themselves that the worthy successor to Chingis Khan was careful to appear impartial, sharing his patronage equally among the religions of his subjects and diplomatically attending all their important ceremonies. His mother Sorkaktani, who had died soon after his election, had been a Christian all her life, but she had set him a judicious example by founding a richly endowed Moslem college in Bukhara.

At the end of May Mangku returned to Karakorum and the friars went with him. William of Rubruck was, therefore, the first European to record his impressions of the Mongol capital. Except for the khan's palace he found it no bigger than the village of Saint Denis outside Paris, and he wrote that even the monastery of Saint Denis was ten times larger than the palace. Nevertheless it was obviously the cosmopolitan capital of a great empire. Archaeological research has revealed that it covered an area of about one and a half square miles with suburbs beyond its four gates and Friar William was probably underestimating its size. It contained twelve Buddhist, Taoist and Shamanist temples, two Moslem mosques, one Nestorian Christian church and palaces for members of the imperial family and court officials. Within its own walls the khan's palace was built in the Chinese style. The court and the separate pavilions stood on raised mounds and were joined to each other by galleries around sheltered courtyards. The coloured tiles on the roofs were glazed and the ridge tiles were shaped like dragons, and the buildings were richly decorated inside with lacquered carvings. The hall where the khan held court, which was a hundred and eighty feet long and nearly a hundred and fifty feet wide, was laid out 'like a church', with a central nave and three rows of seven pillars on either side of it, although in his report Friar William only remembered two rows. Near the entrance to the court there was a new silver drinking fountain designed by Guillaume Buchier, a Parisian master goldsmith who had also provided the magnificent ornaments for the Nestorian church. The fountain was shaped like a tree, with wine and *kumiz* pouring into silver bowls from the mouths of the lions at its feet and the snakes on its branches, and on top there was an angel with a trumpet which could be sounded by a man hidden inside the vault in its base, to summon the cellarers when the wine ran out. There were many European craftsmen working in Karakorum, most of whom had been taken prisoner in Hungary, but Buchier had risen to particular prominence and wealth through the khan's admiration for his artistry. At Mangku's camp a French girl called Paquette had advised the friars to seek him out, and on their first evening in the capital they dined at his house and met his adopted Mongol son, who thereafter became the much-needed replacement for their interpreter.

At Karakorum Friar William preached the gospel, but he was totally unsuited to the missionary task he had set himself. His theology was intolerant and dogmatic and his arguments were academic and philosophical. In desperation he attempted to browbeat his bewildered audiences into embracing his faith by threatening them with hell fire. On more than one occasion Mangku advised him to introduce his new doctrines more gently and simply and suggested that there might possibly be more than one road to heaven, but with no effect. During his entire stay in the capital Friar William's achievement amounted to no more than the conversion to Catholicism of one Nestorian priest on his deathbed and the baptism of six German children. On 30 May he took part in a debate at the palace with representatives of all the other religions. Mangku and his courtiers merely regarded it as an entertainment and after an opening argument between Friar William and the Buddhists on the existence of God, which convinced nobody, the

Moslems declined to take part and the debate dissolved into a carouse.

Disillusioned by the superstitious heresies of the Nestorians and disappointed by his own failure, Friar William prepared to return and report to King Louis on the enormous army that had left for Syria under Hulegu at the end of 1253. For a while he delayed in the hope of learning more about this army's objectives from the Christian King of Little Armenia, who was said to be on his way to Karakorum, but at the beginning of July, when the king had not arrived, he gave up waiting and set out for Russia with a Mongol escort. Friar Bartholomew, who was too sick to travel, was given permission to stay in Karakorum, where he remained for the rest of his life, so becoming the first Catholic missionary to die in the east.

Mangku had wanted to send an ambassador with Friar William, but the friar objected, since, like Friar John, he could not vouch for his safety. Instead the khan gave him a letter for King Louis, which was not quite so arrogant as the letters that had been given to Friar John and Friar Andrew. The khan did not offer to renew the alliance, which he had heard about from Friar William, but he did realize the advantage of remaining on friendly terms with the soldiers who still controlled the Palestinian coast. Thus, although he demanded that Louis should send his ambassadors to make peace and warned him not to contemplate war, or to imagine that his country was too far away to be threatened, his letter did not demand tribute. On the contrary it contained one sentence which was as near as the ruler of the world might be expected to come to an apology. Repudiating responsibility for the rebuff which Friar Andrew had suffered at the hands of Oghul-Ghaimish, he continued: 'How could that wicked woman, viler than a bitch, know about the business of war and peace?'

After resting at Sarai, which Batu was beginning to build into a permanent city, Friar William collected Gosset and travelled south through the Caucasus, where he met five Dominicans who had been sent by the pope to find the German slaves. He persuaded them to abandon what he saw as a hopeless mission. From Armenia he sailed to Cyprus, but on his arrival learned that King Louis had already returned to France. Before he could set out after him, his provincial vicar ordered him to go back to Acre, where he became a lecturer in theology – a position which was obviously more appropriate to his talents than simple evangelism.

The unjustified interference of Friar William's provincial vicar forced him to record his findings in a report which was sent to King Louis towards the end of 1255. His observations about Mongol society were far more detailed than Friar John's. He was the first European to describe the customs and ceremonies of the oriental religions, instead of portraying fabled monsters, he expressed his surprise at not having found any. However, although he reported the army that was advancing against Syria, he did not advocate an alliance with the Mongols, saying: 'Were it allowed me, I would to the utmost of my power preach war against them throughout the whole world.' His own failure had turned missionary ardour into prejudiced pessimism and for all the scholarship that was to make his report a treasure to posterity, at the time it served most to sustain the reticence of Christendom, which was by then no more than fear of the unknown.

In the autumn of 1255 newly-conscripted *tumens* from the empire of the Golden Horde under three of Batu's nephews, Balaghai, Khuli and Tutar, joined the army of Hulegu at its camp outside Samarkand. On 1 January 1256 Hulegu led them across the Amu Darya and the campaign to conquer Syria began. Roads and bridges had been repaired and secured and at the already established camp sites and supply depots, controlled by the vanguard under the Christian *noyan* Ked-Buka, agents were waiting to report. The first objectives were the suppression of the two independent powers which stood on either side of Syria's eastern flank: in the south, the Caliph of Baghdad, who as spiritual ruler of Islam could summon soldiers from the armies of every Moslem prince; and in the north, the Ismaili Order of the Assassins. The Assassins were unsupported by the orthodox Moslems, upon whom their drug-crazed murderers had imposed their political will for nearly two hundred years, and although their mountain fortresses were supposed to be impregnable, they had never faced an army as mighty and competent as Hulegu's, which was over a hundred thousand strong and contained a thousand crews of Chinese bombardiers.

As the walls of his first fortresses began to crumble under the accuracy of the Mongol artillery, the last Master of the Assassins, Rukn ad-Din, sued for peace, in the hope that negotiations would gain him time until winter hampered the assaults. But on 19 November his own commanders advised him to surrender. In return for his life he ordered his strongholds to open their gates and the few that disobeyed were taken by storm. Only the principal fortress at Alamut held out, and when it finally fell after a three-year siege the historian Juvaini, who accompanied the Mongol expedition, examined the library and set aside the copies of the Koran and the books on astronomy before ordering the remaining heresies to be destroyed. By February 1257 over a hundred of the castles of the Assassins had been demolished, their occupants, including the women and children, had been slaughtered; and Juvaini wrote that 'the world was cleansed'. Unable to break his word and execute Rukn ad-Din, Hulegu granted his request to be sent to Karakorum, but when he arrived Mangku refused to receive him, and on the way home he was kicked to death by his guards.

In March 1257 Hulegu set up his headquarters near Hamadan where he was joined by Baiju who, since the execution of Eljigidei, had regained command over the Mongol army of occupation in the west of the empire. It was this army that had originally been entrusted by Kuyuk with the conquest of Syria. Hulegu was furious that Baiju had not already attacked Baghdad as Eljigidei had intended, but Baiju pleaded with some justification that his soldiers had been fully occupied retaining control over the Seljuks in Rum and quelling an uprising in Georgia. With the addition of Baiju's *tumens*, which were now free to join him, and a promised contingent of Christian soldiers from Georgia, the size of Hulegu's army was potentially almost doubled and at the end of the month he sent the first of several letters to the Caliph of Baghdad demanding to know why he had not provided soldiers to assist in the destruction of the Assassins and ordering him to dismantle his walls and come to the camp in person to swear allegiance.

Like the Master of the Assassins, the decadent caliph, Mustasim, prevaricated and his answers were as haughty as Hulegu's demands. He reminded him of the many armies that had failed against Baghdad in the past and advised the 'young man' not to overestimate his good fortune. Since succeeding his father as caliph in 1242 Mustasim had left the administration of the city to self-seeking ministers, and confident in the political prestige of his holy office he had neglected its army. When Hulegu's first letter arrived his military commanders advised him to recruit more soldiers and repair his defences, but his senior minister, the vizier Ibn al-Alkami persuaded him that he was already strong enough to resist until the rest of Islam rallied behind him. Mustasim must have been a very vain and gullible man to have preferred the assurances of his vizier to the obvious arguments of his generals. Baghdad was no longer a powerful city. It was still the spiritual and academic capital of Islam, and it contained the finest university in the world, but its commercial prominence had been lost and the warehouses and bazaars on the west bank of the Tigris were almost deserted. It still had an army of up to fifty thousand men, but neglect and inactivity had left them ill-equipped and indolent. Although, like his more worthy predecessors, the caliph still had the authority to summon soldiers from all the Moslem empires, there were only two of them left, and while his taunting opposition had lost him the loyalty of the Mamluks, the princes of Syria, whom he had supported, were already busy preparing their own defences.

After several exchanges of ambassadors, in which the caliph eventually agreed to pay tribute but refused to swear allegiance, Hulegu lost patience and commanded his armies to converge in four columns on Baghdad. At last the caliph accepted his generals' advice and ordered that the citizens should be armed and trained and the walls of the city repaired, but his orders were delayed by his vizier and it was not until the day before the Mongols arrived that work on the walls began. In the sectarian quarrels that divided Islam, the caliph supported the Sunnites, but his vizier was a Shiite, and resenting the caliph's persecution of some of his Shiite brethren, the vizier had been sending secret messages to the Mongols since the beginning of the negotiations, urging them to attack, describing the city's vulnerability and offering his assistance in the hope that after the city had been taken he might be invited to govern it.

In a gallant but futile gesture twenty thousand men from the caliph's garrison rode out to delay the Mongol advance, but the Mongol soldiers on their flank broke the dykes on the banks of the Tigris, flooding their camp and cutting off their line of retreat. By the time Hulegu's vanguard engaged them many had already been drowned and only a very few survived to return to the city among the throngs of refugees. While Baiju's army occupied the commercial quarter on the west bank of the Tigris, Hulegu was welcomed in the Shiite suburbs beyond the eastern walls and within twenty-four hours the city had been surrounded by a ditch

Chingis Khan, founder of the Mongol empire.

A Persian impression of Chingis Khan in battle.

A Chinese style pavilion
in the Mongol court at
Karakorum.

The bier of Chingis
Khan.

The monastery of Erdeni Tsu near Karakorum. The walls are similar to those which once surrounded the Mongol capital and the imperial palace.

Yurts, which once housed the Mongol army, are still used by herdsmen in the steppes.

ABOVE LEFT A wax impression of a cameo of the Holy Roman Emperor, Frederick II.

ABOVE RIGHT A wooden statue of King Louis IX of France.

A European impression of King Bela IV of Hungary escaping from the Mongols after the Battle of Mohi.

The Mongol army in battle. From a copy of Rashid ad-Din's Compendium made for the Mogul emperor Akbar in the 16th century. The Persian artist has given the horses elaborate caparisons, but the armour and weapons are similar to those used during the western campaigns.

A Mongol horseman today. The saddle and harness have hardly changed.

A Mongol mounted archer.

A Mongol archer using a thumb ring and a composite bow. After a drawing made in China during the reign of Kubilai Khan.

A Mongol *paitze* found near the river Dnieper. The inscription was written in Uighur characters since the Mongols had no alphabet.

Hulegu feasting before advancing to attack the castles of the Assassins.

Detail from a Persian impression of the siege of Baghdad showing one of the Mongol light-weight siege-engines.

and a rampart. On 30 January 1258 the bombardment of Baghdad began.

Until the ammunition trains arrived with rocks from the Jebel Hamrin mountains, three days journey away, the artillery pounded the walls with the trunks of palm trees and stones from the foundations of the suburbs, and arrows carrying messages that promised safety to the civilians if they surrendered were shot into the streets by the archers. Several times during seven days of uninterrupted barrage the caliph sent messengers to offer his submission, but Hulegu was no longer prepared to accept anything less than unconditional surrender. By the morning of 6 February, the bombardment was over and the Mongols had stormed and captured the entire eastern wall.

For another seven days the Mongol soldiers remained on the wall while the city surrendered. First Hulegu sent a messenger calling on the soldiers in the garrison to lay down their arms and abandon their posts and, believing that they would be allowed to retire into Syria, they marched out unarmed, only to be divided into companies and slaughtered. Then the caliph came out to surrender with his three sons and three thousand courtiers. They were taken prisoner, but those citizens who were persuaded to follow them met the same fate as their garrison. Not until 13 February did Hulegu give the signal for the sack of Baghdad. The Christians who assembled in the Nestorian church and some of the foreign visitors were spared, but the Moslem population was subjected to a hideous massacre, in which the Christian soldiers of Georgia took part with particular relish, and when all were dead and the plunder had been removed, the mosques and palaces were set on fire. The contents of the caliph's fabulous treasure house were loaded into two huge wagon trains and sent to Mangku at Karakorum or to the island of Shalia in Lake Urmiya where the fort that Hulegu built to house them was later to become his tomb. During the week of slaughter and pillage Hulegu held a banquet with the caliph in his palace, at which he pretended that his prisoner was his host and mocked him for not having used his treasure to pay soldiers to defend him. When his beautiful city was in ruins, the caliph and his sons were sewn up in carpets and trampled to death beneath the hooves of Mongol horses. His vizier retained his office, but only survived the caliph for three months. Some said that he died of a broken heart: according to the Shiites it was because his city had been destroyed and according to the Sunnites because he had not been invited to govern its ruins. To Moslem historians the destruction of Baghdad was such a calamity that the numbers of the dead were hysterically overestimated at between eight hundred thousand and two million; yet, including the refugees there must have been several hundred thousand people in the city when it fell, and not for the first time the Mongol armies were forced to abandon their camps by the stench of the corpses.

To many Moslem princes resistance seemed hopeless after the fall of Baghdad and while Hulegu led his armies north through Hamadam to rest and re-equip at winter quarters near Tabriz, they came to his camp one by one to offer their submission. Among them was the Prince of Mosul, who had once made the rash vow that he would take the Mongol conqueror by the ears. To the amusement of his ministers he fulfilled it by offering Hulegu a pair of gold earrings and humbly requesting that he should be allowed to put them on the khan's ears himself. Kai-Kawus and Kilij-Arslan, the two rival rulers of Rum, between whom the sultanate, like the kingdom of Georgia, had been divided by its Mongol overlords, also came to renew their allegiance. Kai-Kawus, who had attempted to defy the Mongols and had been defeated in battle by Baiju, was so afraid of Hulegu's wrath that as a mark of his contrition and servility he presented him with a pair of socks that had his portrait painted on the soles, so that his master might walk on his face. The most important visitor, however, was the son of the Sultan of Syria, who came to make peace on behalf of his father. Since the failure of his attack on Egypt, the Syrian sultan, al-Nasir, had achieved an uneasy truce with the Mamluks, which had been negotiated by the caliph and by which he had been forced to cede Jerusalem and Gaza. Doubting therefore that the Mamluks would support him, and terrified by the advance of Hulegu's army, he had already sent rich tribute to Mangku at Karakorum. The letter which his son was given to take back to Aleppo was composed for Hulegu by the astronomer Nasir ad-Din, for whom Hulegu had ordered a new observatory to be built at Maragha. The letter was said to have been a masterpiece of Arabic style, filled with irony, flamboyant imagery and sarcastic quotations from the Koran; and it demanded no less than total surrender. The lesser Moslem princes had been received courteously and granted the privilege of providing soldiers for the Mongol army, but the Sultan of

Syria was warned that he was 'doomed to misfortune and to fall'.

The Syrian Christians, however, rejoiced when they learned that the five-hundred-year-old capital of Islam was in ruins. To them it seemed as though the prophesied armies of Prester John were on their way at last and that when Hulegu's soldiers crossed the Euphrates, Saint John the Divine's vision of Armageddon would come true. Hulegu was a Buddhist, but he was as impartial in matters of religion as his brother Mangku, and although he manipulated sectarian animosities to divide his enemies, it was the Christians who exercised the greatest influence on his policies: Ked-Buka, who had become his favourite commander, was a Christian and so was his senior wife Dokuz-Khatun. It was the polygamous Mongol tradition for sons to marry their fathers' widows, with the exception of their own mother, and Dokuz-Khatun, who was a niece of Wang Khan, had been a wife to Hulegu's father. She was a devout Nestorian and always had a chapel next to her tent where she said mass every day; and since the beginning of the campaign her charity had earned her a saintly reputation. So great was Mangku's respect for her that he had commanded his brother always to consult her and abide by her advice. Furthermore, during his visit to Karakorum, King Hayton of Little Armenia had persuaded Mangku that it would be to his strategic advantage to represent the conquest of Syria as a crusade and had obtained from him the promise that, after they had been taken, the Holy Places would be returned to the Christians. If Friar William had stayed longer in the Mongol capital, King Louis' crusaders might have been offered a more reliable alliance.

Hulegu's letter had left the Sultan of Syria with little choice, since surrender meant certain death, but the Mongol campaigns of the previous year had crippled his empire with famine, plague and panic, and with the addition of more *tumens* from Mosul and the other new Moslem vassals and a token contingent of sixteen thousand soldiers from Little Armenia, Hulegu's army was now well over three hundred thousand strong. In desperation the Sultan of Syria turned to the Mamluks, but in Cairo the new sultan was Aybak's fifteen-year-old son Ali and Egypt was under the regency of the Mamluk commander Kutuz: after discovering that Aybak intended to murder her, Shajar al-Durr had allowed her supporters to murder him first and had then been beaten to death

herself by his former wife and her slave girls. Kutuz had no intention of helping al-Nasir in Syria, but when his letter arrived, he
used it to his own advantage. Declaring that in such an emergency
it was dangerous for Egypt to be ruled by a boy, he put Ali into
prison and had himself proclaimed as the new Mamluk sultan.

On 12 September 1259, after receiving a hopelessly defiant letter
from the Syrian sultan al-Nasir, Hulegu advanced and, leaving
Aleppo under the command of his uncle, Turan Shah, al-Nasir
fled to Damascus. Before the Mongols crossed the Euphrates, a
detachment, made up mostly of Georgians and Armenians, was
sent to attack Maijyfarakin, where the treacherous prince Kamil
Muhammad, who had sworn allegiance to Mangku, had provided
soldiers for the caliph and crucified a Jacobite priest who was
travelling through his city on a Mongol passport. When the city
fell, pieces were cut from Kamil's flesh and forcibly fed to him till
he died. At Aleppo, as at Baghdad, part of the garrison rode out and
was destroyed in an ambush and, after a week of bombardment, the
city was taken by storm on 20 January 1260. While the citadel held
out for another four weeks, the city was razed to the ground, the
women and children were taken away into slavery and, with the
exception of a few traitors and those who had been given shelter in
the synagogue, the Moslem men were slaughtered. After the citadel
had fallen Turan Shah was spared; the Mongols' admiration for so
much courage in an old man had earned him the rest of his life.

When the sultan learned that Aleppo was lost, he fled from
Damascus. Panic in Syria had reached such a pitch that even
princes were selling everything that they owned for a fraction of
its value, and a few camels could cost as much as a ship. Most of
the sultan's officers, disillusioned by his lack of determination, had
deserted him on the pretext that they were escorting the wife and
treasure that he had sent to Cairo, and while some dauntless
citizens were preparing an embassy to surrender Damascus to
Hulegu, their sultan travelled towards Egypt. Near Gaza, however,
he changed his mind. The Mamluks had not answered his plea for
help and he feared rightly that his pretensions to the throne in
Cairo would lead them to murder him. He turned back, and, like
Muhammad II of Khwarizm, became a fugitive in his own empire.

At Aleppo, Hulegu was within striking distance of the crusaders'
states on the Palestinian coast and all their commanders realized
that it was only a matter of time before there would be no indepen-

dent Moslem power east of Morocco. But only a few in Acre, including Anno von Sangerhausen, the Grand Master of the Teutonic Knights, who had accompanied King Louis's disastrous crusade, argued that they might recover some of their losses by supporting the Mongols. The majority believed that an attack was inevitable and they wrote to King Louis's brother, Charles of Anjou, begging him to reinforce them. In the north, however, Count Bohemund of Antioch and Tripoli, who controlled all the coast north of Beirut, was more optimistic. He was the son-in-law of King Hayton of Little Armenia and like Hayton believed that the Mongols would keep their word. When Hayton rode down to join Hulegu after the fall of Aleppo, Bohemund came too and brought with him his army of crusaders, who were to become the only western European soldiers ever to march beside the Mongols.

Count Bohemund's faith proved justified. Hulegu returned to him all the lands west of Aleppo that had once belonged to Antioch, and, to the horror of the church of Rome, Bohemund agreed to replace the Catholic patriarch of Antioch with a representative of the Greek Orthodox church, in accordance with Hulegu's policy of sectarian impartiality.

At the beginning of February, after the ambassadors from Damascus had surrendered the keys of their city and returned with a promise of amnesty, Hulegu, King Hayton and Count Bohemund began to plan the offensive that would return Jerusalem to the Christians. Then came news of the one event that could halt their advance: on 12 August 1259 Mangku Khan had died of dysentery. At once Hulegu withdrew the bulk of his army into Azerbaijan and the campaign was postponed.

Just as the death of Ogedei had saved Christendom, the death of Mangku saved Islam. But Hulegu's position was far more precarious than Batu's had been. As he had wished, Mangku's brother Kubilai had been proclaimed khan in China, but another brother, Arik-Boke, had engineered his own election in Karakorum, and for the first time the supreme khanate of the Mongol Empire was being contested on the battlefield. Since Arik-Boke had given the empire of Chagatai's family around Transoxiana and Kara Khitai to Alghu, the one grandson of Chagatai who was prepared to support him, Hulegu was afraid that he, Arik-Boke, might find another puppet and make a similar disposition of his own empire. Above all, Batu was dead and the Golden Horde was now ruled by his

brother Berke, who was a Moslem. Berke had been piously horrified by the destruction of Baghdad and it was only his loyalty to
Mangku that had prevented him from withdrawing the *tumens* of
the Golden Horde from Hulegu's army. But there was nothing to
stop him now and, to make matters worse, the subject peoples of
the Golden Horde, who provided the bulk of its army, were not
only members of the same race as the Mamluks, but in many cases
were also members of the same families. Isolated and surrounded
by potential enemies, Hulegu could do nothing but hang on to the
heart of his empire and wait.

Ked-Buka was left behind to control the new conquests in Syria.
He raided as far south as Gaza and the sultan was captured near
Amman and sent to Hulegu's camp where he was executed. But
'the crusade' was over, and its only achievement had been the
return to Christendom of Damascus. One of the mosques became a
church and on 1 March the European Count Bohemund, the
Middle Eastern King Hayton and the oriental *noyan* Ked-Buka
rode side by side in triumph through the streets, while the Moslem
population bowed before the cross that was carried ahead of them.
It was a poignant image of a Christian world that so nearly might
have been.

It was the campaign in Syria that saved Europe from another
invasion. In Russia the census and subsequent conscription that
provided a flow of new *tumens* for Hulegu's army deprived the
Golden Horde of the soldiers who would otherwise have been used
to support a full scale offensive in the west. But while some of the
crusaders in Acre contemplated an alliance, there was one short
period in 1259 when the people of eastern Europe were reminded
that the Mongols were their potential conquerors.

When Batu died in 1255, Sartak ruled for less than a year and
was succeeded by his brother Ulaghchi, to whom the Russian
princes were required to renew their allegiance. On the instigation
of Alexander Nevsky, his brother Andrew returned repentant from
Sweden with such magnificent tribute that he was restored to the
Grand Duchy of Suzdal. But this time it was Daniel of Galicia who
rebelled. He believed that while so many *tumens* were being supplied and equipped for the war in Syria the numbers and resources
of the occupying armies were severely stretched, and in this he saw
his last chance of freedom. He had lost faith in the papacy, but he
had found a new ally in the Lithuanian Prince Mendovg. The

pagan Lithuanians, who had been raiding Galicia and Volynia for many years, had been driven eastwards into 'Black Russia' by the advances of the Teutonic Knights, and to protect himself Mendovg, like Daniel, had undergone token conversion to Catholicism, for which he too had been rewarded with a crown. Doubting the reliability of the pope and his German crusaders, he had also made an alliance with his former Galician enemy, by which the widower Daniel had married his niece and Daniel's son Roman had been given his own estates in Mendovg's domains. Supported by Mendovg, Daniel drove the Mongol outposts out of eastern Volynia and when Khurumsi, who commanded the Mongol army west of the Dnieper, led a small expedition into Galicia and Volynia, the rebels retired into the fortified cities and without the strength either to besiege or to storm them, Khurumsi was forced to withdraw. Daniel's success was, however, short-lived. In 1258 Ulaghchi died and was succeeded by Batu's resolute brother Berke, who replaced Khurumsi with Burundai, gave him reinforcements and sent him to punish the rebels with an army of thirty thousand men. At the same time, Mendovg, realizing that the Mongols were a far more uncompromising and formidable enemy than the Teutonic Knights, withdrew his support and arrested Daniel's son Roman. Burundai was cunning. He attacked the more powerful Lithuanians and sent a threatening request for assistance to Daniel. Afraid that he would be punished, Daniel sent his brother Vasilko to Burundai's camp to agree and only joined in the campaign himself with his son Leo when the invasion of the Lithuanian lands began. By clever manoeuvring Mendovg avoided a major engagement in the field and the Russian soldiers failed to find Daniel's son Roman, but the lands were laid waste and the towns were plundered. In 1259, when the campaign was over, Burundai turned his attention to Galicia and Volynia. The cities were compelled to demolish their defences and Daniel, still frightened of a reprisal, discreetly withdrew through Poland into Hungary, where he remained until Burundai's army had gone.

While Burundai was in Volynia, a detachment of the Mongol army, accompanied by some of the Russian soldiers, crossed the border into Poland. Perhaps they were looking for Daniel, but he was not punished when he returned, and it may have been simply that the suppression of the Lithuanians had renewed the Mongol taste for plunder. It seems more likely, however, that their purpose was to ensure that Galicia and Volynia's neighbours would not be tempted to support any future rebellion, particularly since they offered an alliance to King Bela of Hungary and invited him to join them. The objectives of the campaign in 1241 had been purely strategic and this time the destruction was far more terrible. Once again Duke Boleslaw fled to Hungary; Sandomir and Lublin were sacked and their citizens massacred; although the citadel held out, the rest of Cracow, which had only just been rebuilt, was returned to ashes; and all the lands and villages of northern Poland as far as the borders of Oppeln were devastated. Horrified but helpless, the new pope, Alexander IV, implored King Bela to defend the Poles and warned him not to make an alliance with the heathens, but Bela, who supported neither the Poles nor the Mongols, replied derisively that it was ridiculous to threaten him with a power that had been so ineffective when the Mongols were his enemies. Within three months of their attack the Mongol raiders returned to Russia unopposed.

After the raid, Alexander IV proclaimed a crusade against the Mongols and in 1260 he excommunicated Count Bohemund for supporting them in Syria. But he was no more able to muster an army of crusaders than his predecessors had been. When Pope Innocent IV and the Emperor Frederick's son Conrad both died in 1254, Alexander and the emperor's illegitimate son Manfred had continued their war and Europe was still divided. No one was prepared to advance into Russia, while only a few set sail for the Holy Land, and, although the crusaders in Acre had sent their plea for help to Charles of Anjou, who as a contender for the throne of the Holy Roman Empire was anxious to ingratiate himself with the pope, even he preferred to restrict the pursuit of his ambitions to Europe. It was on the basis of this European impotence and the experience of Count Bohemund that, among the crusaders in Acre, the Grand Master of the Teutonic Knights argued that an alliance with the Mongols was still in their best interest, but the proclamation of a crusade and the excommunication of Count Bohemund convinced the majority that such an alliance would lead to European reprisals and their own excommunication. When Hulegu withrew the bulk of his army from Syria, however, their apprehension was diminished and two of their more reckless commanders, Julian of Sidon and John of Beirut, led independent raids into Mongol-occupied Gaza and Galilee, in the first of which Ked-

Buka's nephew was killed. The resulting retaliation, in which Ked-Buka sacked Sidon and John of Beirut's army of Templars was decimated on the battlefield, renewed their anxiety. Having underestimated and angered the Mongols, the isolated crusaders were beginning to accept that, whatever the cost, only an un-hallowed alliance would ensure their survival, when a messenger arrived from Cairo with a surprising and far less dependable proposal.

Before the news of Mangku's death reached Aleppo, Hulegu had written the usual Mongol declaration of war to the Mamluks, demanding the surrender of Egypt and threatening an invasion if they refused. Courageous and accomplished though they were, the Mamluks did not have the numerical strength to withstand an army as large as Hulegu's and at the time it seemed that their fall was inevitable. Yet soon after the letter arrived they learned that Hulegu had begun to evacuate most of his soldiers from Syria and furthermore, since the death of Mangku, Berke had ordered the *tumens* of the Golden Horde to return to Russia. The sultan, Kutuz, summoned a council of his generals and, like several deter-mined commanders before him, committed them to war by executing the Mongol ambassadors and nailing their heads to one of the gates of Cairo. The Mamluk generals were ready to defend their new empire, but they were afraid that the invaders might still be too powerful if Ked-Buka joined forces with the crusaders and only a few were prepared to support Kutuz's plan to advance deep into Syria and destroy Ked-Buka's army before Hulegu returned. Exasperated, Kutuz stormed out of the council, declaring that if no one would come with him he would go and fight the Mongols alone, and he wrote to the crusaders offering an alliance and asking that he should at least be granted a truce and safe conduct to lead his soldiers north through the coastal remnants of the Kingdom of Jerusalem, and then turn east into Syria to take Ked-Buka in the flank.

The astonished crusaders vacillated. Some saw the Moslem army as the defenders of civilization, while others, led by the Grand Master of the Teutonic Knights, still believed that the Mongols were the better allies for the Christian cause. Nevertheless the majority were eager for revenge after the sack of Sidon, and the grand master's arguments served only to deter them from offering military support. Eventually they agreed to grant safe conduct and provide supplies, and invited Kutuz and his staff to dine with them when they marched past Acre. It was a decision that was to be fatal for the future of Christianity in Asia.

Kutuz combined the energy and charisma of a conqueror with the eloquence of an orator. The Mamluks rallied and on 26 July 1260 their vanguard left Cairo under the command of Baybars. When the news reached Ked-Buka he prepared to march down to meet them, but the Moslems in Damascus revolted, murdering Christians and burning their houses, and he delayed until the rebellion was quelled. Meanwhile the Mamluks turned north through the lands of the crusaders and camped near Acre. As promised, the crusaders supplied them and gave a banquet for their commanders, and when they returned to their camp Baybars impetuously announced that he could take the city easily, but Kutuz reminded him that for the time being they had a more dangerous enemy. There were a hundred and twenty thousand men under their command: the ranks had been swollen by fugitives from all the defeated Moslem armies and the few soldiers of the Golden Horde who had not yet returned to Russia had received new orders to join them. Kutuz assembled them, and after delivering a rousing speech in which he recalled the atrocities of the Mongol campaigns and exhorted them to save their families from a similar fate or die in the attempt, he led them south-east past Nazareth towards the river Jordan.

Ked-Buka left Damascus with a Christian army of twenty-five thousand Mongols, Georgians and Armenians. He knew that the Mamluks had reached Acre and he knew the size of their army, but he was a Mongol general and he was not impressed by numbers. At dawn on 3 September 1260 he crossed the river Jordan and rode ten miles along the Plain of Esdraelon between the mountains of Gilboa and the hills of Galilee, into the valley where David slew Goliath. Here, near the village of Ain Jalut (Goliath's Spring), he met the Mamluk vanguard advancing under Baybars.

At the first Mongol charge the Mamluk vanguard broke. Baybars fled up the valley and Ked-Buka gave chase, but the Mongols were falling for their own trick. In the hills beyond there were men who had fought against them before on the Russian steppes and even some who had fought beside them. Nevertheless Kutuz was too cautious to attack the Mongol flanks. Instead he drew up his soldiers across the four miles of the valley ahead of them. Ked-Buka, realizing that he had committed himself to engaging the entire Mamluk army, checked and signalled the 'standard sweep'. His front ranks drove into the retreating vanguard as it reached its lines, while the rest wheeled right towards the hills of Galilee and bore down on the wing. Baybars escaped, but the Mamluk vanguard was destroyed and the left wing crumbled. For most of the morning Kutuz strove desperately to regain his flank, moving men across from his right wing and countercharging recklessly to cover them. Eventually the Mamluks were again on either side of the Mongols and the moment had come for Kutuz to chance everything on his numerical superiority. Taking off his helmet so that his men might recognize him, he rode out in front with his bodyguard and led the massed charge of the Mamluks. The Mongol army was overwhelmed. Ked-Buka refused to retreat and galloped backwards and forwards in front of his men shouting that it was their duty to die where they stood. One chronicle records that he was killed in the Mamluk charge and another that when his horse was shot from under him he was led before Kutuz and executed. When he fell, his soldiers retreated for eight miles to the small town of Beisan where they made a second stand, but that too was swept away and the survivors fled across the Jordan. Ked-Buka's head was carried back to Cairo by the messenger who brought news of the Mamluk victory and a week later Kutuz entered Damascus in triumph.

The battle of Ain Jalut has been recorded as one of the most decisive and significant battles in the history of the world. It was not a conclusive victory in itself and it was no dishonour to Georgian, Armenian and Mongol arms that the soldiers fought so well against such odds, but it destroyed the myth of the Mongols' invincibility, it broke the momentum of their conquests and it marked the day when Islam was returned towards triumph from the brink of oblivion. From that time onwards, while confusion and discord divided their enemies, the Mamluks flourished, the final methodical expulsion of the crusaders from Palestine began and Christian influence in Asia was eclipsed.

11
The End of an Era

FOR four years after the death of Mangku Khan, his brothers Kubilai and Arik-Boke fought for his throne and before their conflict was resolved, the two khans of the western empires were also at war with each other. The unity that had made the Mongols omnipotent was lost. Berke supported Arik-Boke and Hulegu supported Kubilai; Berke was a devout Moslem and Hulegu was an infidel who favoured the Christians; but, although these separate loyalties had divided them, it was envy that made them enemies. Berke claimed that since Chingis Khan had bequeathed all the western conquests to his father, Hulegu's new empire in Georgia, Azerbaijan and Rum was rightfully his, and when the Mamluks offered him a firm alliance he saw his chance to take it.

Daunted by the size of Hulegu's army, the Mamluks withdrew from Syria at the beginning of October 1260, but by the end of the year Kutuz had been replaced by Baybars, the glamorous young conqueror who was to become the greatest of the Mamluk sultans. On 25 October the army camped a few miles from Cairo and the soldiers spent the day hunting while the city was decorated for their triumphal entry. Kutuz had quarrelled with Baybars and, alarmed by his prestige and ambition, he had refused to make him governor of Aleppo, but they were riding side by side like friends when, at a prearranged signal, one of Baybars's supporters struck Kutuz with his sword while another pulled him from his horse, and as he lay wounded on the ground, Baybars drew his bow and shot him dead. That night, before the news could spread, Baybars occupied the citadel of Cairo and next day he was proclaimed and accepted as sultan.

Baybars was personally reckless, but his strategies were cautious and his diplomacy was cunning. He always knew that Hulegu's armies were too strong for him and he dreaded an alliance between the Mongols and the crusaders, yet during his reign the Mamluk empire of Egypt and Syria was to become the most powerful Moslem state in the Middle East and the crusaders were to lose most of their strongholds in Palestine. If the Mongol armies in Persia had not been preoccupied and if enough of the crusaders had dared to trust them, Baybars would never have achieved this power. Before he led the Mamluks back into Syria, he sent an Alan merchant to Sarai with a letter urging Berke to wage war against his infidel cousin in the name of Islam. Berke agreed, and by the beginning of 1262 the Khan of the Golden Horde and the Mamluk Sultan of Egypt were exchanging ambassadors through Constantinople. In the spring Baybars attacked Hulegu's Christian ally in Antioch and in the summer Berke sent an army across the Caucasus to invade Georgia.

Neither the rivalry in the imperial family, nor Berke's Moslem cause, would have been enough to persuade his commanders that they should attack another Mongol army, particularly since some of them were Christians. Furthermore, after the successful raid in Poland, many were eager to attempt another invasion of Europe. But two of the princes who had led Berke's *tumens* under Hulegu had mysteriously disappeared and, on the probably correct assumption that they had been murdered, Berke convinced his *noyans* that the campaign was to be no more than traditional Mongol retribution. Accordingly, command of the avenging army was given to another nephew called Nogai. Berke was unable to lead the expedition himself or to assign to it as many *tumens* as it required because the cities of Suzdalia had rebelled against their tax collectors and he was preparing a punitive expedition, but he was anxious to conquer as much of Hulegu's empire as he could before the war in the east was over. If Arik-Boke were to emerge victorious, he would undoubtedly recognize the lawful claim, but if it were to be Kubilai, he would be unlikely to accept anything less than a *fait accompli*.

Nogai crossed the Caucasus, occupied Derbend and advanced into Shirvan, but Hulegu had come north to meet him. His outnumbered army was driven back, Derbend was stormed and when Nogai retreated through the pass beyond it, Hulegu's son Abaka was sent after him. In the steppes, however, Nogai was reinforced by Berke with the army that had been reserved for Suzdalia. After quelling the rebels and giving his own assurances for their future obedience, Alexander Nevsky, whose conciliatory policies had

already saved so much of Russia from devastation, had persuaded
Berke to forgive them, so leaving him free to support his nephews.
It was to be Alexander's last diplomatic achievement: on the way
home from Sarai, he died in Gorodets. On 13 January 1263,
Abaka's soldiers were feasting in Nogai's abandoned camp when
they were surprised and overwhelmed by Berke's army. Abaka
escaped, but most of the routed fugitives were drowned in the river
Terek when the ice broke beneath them. Berke advanced to
Derbend and on the news of his son's defeat Hulegu withdrew to
Tabriz and began to prepare for a major offensive.

During this brief campaign, Baybars had not felt secure enough
to engage in a prolonged siege against any of the crusaders' strongholds, but when he had burned the crops and razed the villages
around Antioch, he made a similar raid on Hulegu's other
Christian ally in Little Armenia, and soon after Hulegu's return to
Tabriz, he destroyed the farms that fed Acre and burned the
Christian church in Nazareth. Hoping that this might at last pro-
voke a Christian alliance, Hulegu sent an embassy to Rome where
the new pope, Urban IV, had succeeded Alexander IV in 1261. In
terms that were humble for the representative of a Mongol khan,
the ambassador pleaded for a combined crusade, but Urban
offered him no more than praise for his master's tolerance, and by
the time the ambassador returned, Hulegu was dead.

Hulegu's invasion of Russia had been delayed by a rebellion in
Mosul and he had been disappointed by the expected support from
the east, since after the defeat of Arik-Boke in 1264, Kaidu had
risen in his place and Kubilai could only afford to spare three
tumens, but by the time Hulegu died on 8 February 1265, his army
was ready to attack. As soon as news of his death reached Sarai,
Berke made a pre-emptive invasion of Georgia with over two
hundred thousand men and Hulegu's heir Abaka advanced to meet
him. After a skirmish between their vanguards, Abaka withdrew to
a defensive position on the left bank of the Kura and for two
weeks the massive Mongol armies manoeuvred and sniped at each
other across the river until, while travelling towards Tiflis to find a
ford, Berke also died and his soldiers returned with his body to
Russia. Abaka left an army in Georgia and built fortifications along
the left bank of the Kura, but there was no need for them. Berke
was succeeded by Batu's grandson, Mangku-Temur, and although
he maintained the Mamluk alliance, he did not share his uncle's

ambitions in Persia and, like Abaka, he recognized Kubilai as the supreme khan.

Abaka was now free to turn his attentions to Syria and since Pope Urban had been succeeded by Clement IV, he sent another ambassador to Europe. But the pope insisted that he should be baptized, while the Christian rulers still believed that once the Mamluks were defeated the Mongols would turn against them, and Baybars's continuing success in Palestine had made them so apprehensive that even the dedicated crusader King Louis was planning to attack Tunis instead. The only man who was prepared to trust them was Prince Edward, the son and heir of King Henry III of England.

Prince Edward did not reach the Holy Land until the spring of 1271 and on his arrival at Acre he sent three representatives, Godfrey Wells, Reginald Russell and John Parker, calling on Abaka to join him, but by then Abaka was defending his eastern frontier against the supporters of Kaidu in Transoxiana who had invaded Khurasan to cut him off from Kubilai. Meanwhile in Palestine the crusaders had been reduced to defending their last fortresses on the edge of the sea. After capturing the port of Jaffa, the famous castle at Krak des Chevaliers and the city of Antioch, Baybars was now attacking Count Bohemund's other stronghold at Tripoli. The Anglo-Mongol alliance was consequently a fiasco: Baybars withdrew his army and stationed it at Damascus, between the allies; Abaka sent only one *tumen*, which drove the Mamluk garrison out of Aleppo and was then called back to the eastern front; and with no more than three hundred knights and a thousand men, Prince Edward was forced to sign a truce and return to England.

However, when his eastern boundaries were secure, Abaka tried again. This time he sent sixteen ambassadors to Europe, among them a Nestorian bishop and an English Dominican called David of Ashby who had been sent to his father Hulegu's court on an exploratory embassy fifteen years before by Pope Alexander IV and had remained among the Mongols ever since. By now there was yet another pope in Rome, Gregory X, but Gregory believed in the Mongol alliance and, by an extraordinary coincidence, he had already sent his own ambassadors to Kubilai Khan. As Tedaldo Visconti, Archbishop of Liège, Pope Gregory had accompanied Prince Edward's crusade and while he was in Acre he had met two

Venetian merchants, Niccolo and Maffeo Polo, who were making their second journey to China. They told him that Kubilai Khan had given them letters for the pope inviting him to send some oil from the lamp in the Holy Sepulchre at Jerusalem and 'a hundred men learned in the Christian religion' to refute the philosophers at his court, but on returning to Italy they found that Pope Clement was dead and after two years in which no new pope was elected, they gave up waiting and set out again for China. When the Polos had left Acre to continue their journey, Tedaldo received the unexpected news that he had been chosen as Clement's successor and messengers were sent galloping to call them back. They were given letters of greeting, but since Acre could not provide a hundred missionaries, only two were selected. Nevertheless, by the time the new pope reached Rome, his ambassadors were already on their way to China.

The war between the papacy and the descendants of Frederick II had at last been ended by a victory for the papacy: Manfred had died in 1266 and in 1268 Charles of Anjou had captured and executed Frederick's grandson Conradin. Pope Gregory was in a better position to rally an army of crusaders than his predecessors had been. When the Mongol ambassadors addressed the Fourteenth Ecumenical Council at Lyons in 1274, with David of Ashby as their interpreter, a new crusade was proclaimed against the Mamluks. The ambassadors returned to Abaka with a promise that representatives would follow them to plan the campaign and in the next three years Abaka sent further emissaries to Rome and even to England, where Edward was now king. But, although the pope was enthusiastic, the men who would have led and paid for the crusade were not, and it all came to nothing. King Louis had died in Tunis in 1270; his brother Charles of Anjou was more interested in recapturing Constantinople from the Greek Orthodox emperor Michael VIII; Edward I of England was busy fighting the Welsh; central Europe was in anarchy; and the merchant communities, particularly the great Italian trading cities, were anxious to remain on good terms with the Mamluks and their allies in the Golden Horde who controlled the northern and southern trade routes to the east. Even the embassy to Kubilai failed: the two friars lost heart and the only member of their party to reach China for the first time was Niccolo Polo's seventeen-year-old son Marco.

Meanwhile Baybars's success continued. Taxation was heavy,

but with the trade routes open Syria was growing rich again and the ruined cities were being rebuilt. Forty new war galleys had been provided for the Egyptian fleet and the well-trained Mamluk army had grown to over two hundred thousand strong. In 1275 Baybars made a more thorough attack on Little Armenia, where Hayton had abdicated in favour of his son Leo, and the cities and ports were destroyed. In 1277 he invaded Rum, defeating the Mongol army of occupation on 16 April at Albistan in terrain so mountainous that both armies fought on foot, and on 23 April he took possession of the capital at Caesarea. But it was to be his last victory. When he heard that Abaka was advancing with his entire army, he cautiously retreated to Antioch. Two months later, at a banquet in Damascus, he became violently sick, and after three days of agony the saviour of Islam died on 20 June 1277, at the age of fifty.

In the same year Pope Gregory died and Abaka abandoned all hope of a crusade, but the brief, incompetent rule of Baybars's two sons and the rebellion in Damascus after the Mamluk commander, Kilawan, had been proclaimed as sultan in their place tempted him to attack alone. When an exploratory expedition succeeded in sacking Aleppo in 1280, he prepared a major offensive and in 1281 he invaded. The spearhead of his attack, directed against Damascus, was an army of fifty thousand Mongols, supported by thirty thousand Georgians and Armenians and led by his young brother, who shared the name Mangku-Temur with the Khan of the Golden Horde. News of the army's approach reached Damascus well ahead of it and Kilawan had time to assemble a force of equal strength and advance. Mamluk communications were even faster than the Mongols': where the Mongols used semaphore and galloping messengers, the Mamluks used carrier pigeons. Mongol intelligence, however, was far superior; they penetrated the Mamluk spy network on the east of the Euphrates and arranged for a carrier pigeon to be sent to Damascus warning Kilawan that the Mongol battle plan would be to concentrate their attack on his right. On 31 October 1281, when the two armies met near the town of Hims, the Mongols' front ranks engaged the front and strengthened right of the Mamluk army, while the rear ranks moved round behind them and launched the main attack against the Mamluk left. On the first impact the left wing broke and its soldiers fled towards Hims, but the victorious Mongol right wing set out after them, abandoning the battlefield, and meanwhile the remainder of the Mamluk army held its ground. As the Mongols prepared for a second charge and the Mamluks reformed their ranks to meet it, a Mamluk officer rode up to the Mongol lines, pretending that he was a deserter, and asked to speak to the Mongol commander. In the heat of battle nobody remembered to disarm him and when he was led before Mangku-Temur, he struck him in the face with his sword. In the confusion that followed the Mamluks charged. Without delegating his command, the wounded prince allowed his staff officers to lead him from the field and when the Mongol soldiers saw his standard withdrawing they turned and followed it. The Mamluks took them in the rear and by the time the *tumens* of the right wing returned from Hims the battle was over and they were ambushed. More soldiers died in the flight than had been killed on the battlefield, and it is to Abaka's incomprehensible discredit that he left the conduct of such a vital mission to so inexperienced a commander, while he devoted his own time to nothing more important than supervising the siege of Rahba on the Euphrates.

The reversal of fortunes at Ain Jalut was confirmed by the victory at Hims, and west of the Euphrates the rule of the Mamluks was secure. When Abaka died in April 1282, five months after the battle, his Moslem brother Taghudar, who adopted the name Ahamad, ruled until he was dethroned in 1284 by Abaka's Buddhist son Argun, and for seven years after that negotiations with Europe continued. But the Mongol ambassadors returned from the popes and the western kings with no more than empty promises and by the time Argun died on 9 April 1291, he had lost all hope of a Christian alliance and the Christian kings had lost all interest in Palestine: six days before, on 3 April, the crusaders' last stronghold at Acre had fallen to the Mamluks. Among the Mongols the influence of Islam inevitably increased, and when Argun's son Ghazan seized the throne in 1295, he achieved it only by renouncing his Buddhism and embracing the Moslem religion of his supporters.

For want of an army and through lack of trust, Christianity had relinquished western Asia to Islam and through the paucity of its missionaries the east was to be lost to Buddhism. Unlike the descendants of Hulegu, Kubilai and his family had no political need to adopt the Taoist religion of their Chinese subjects who, took no part in the higher levels of imperial government and were treated as second-class citizens, forbidden to marry Mongols or learn their language. Kubilai Khan did not share his grandfather's admiration for their learned mandarins. Instead he feared and suspected them and consequently the members of his council were all foreigners: his ministers were Moslems, Nestorians or Buddhists from the western empire and for a while his 'roving secretary of state' was the Catholic Christian Marco Polo. But he never received his hundred missionaries. The few who were sent, like John of Monte Corvino, who became Archbishop of Peking and an imperial official, demonstrated what might have been achieved, but even with the support of the Nestorians, they were too few to stem the flood of Buddhism, which appealed to both the philosophy of the Chinese and the simple culture of their Mongol masters. With the emergence of the Dominicans and the Franciscans, the thirteenth century was an age of renewed and enthusiastic evangelism, yet the greatest opportunities, created by the successes of a pagan empire, were wasted.

In Russia, under the influence of the Mamluk alliance, the Golden Horde became Moslem. Architects from Egypt built mosques in the Crimean ports and in the splendid city of New Sarai, or Berke's Sarai, which was built on the Volga about a hundred and fifty miles north of the old capital and which became a flourishing centre of trade between Europe and the east. From the Crimea, merchant ships sailed to Italy through Constantinople where the Greek emperor, Michael VIII, had been forced to accept an alliance after his lands had been devastated by an army of Mongols and Bulgars under Nogai, but the Venetians lost their monopoly and the Genoese became the predominant European merchants in Russia. In 1261 Michael VIII had recaptured the Byzantine capital from crusaders who had been financed by Venice, and when his throne was secure he gave the sole right of passage through the Bosphorus to Genoa. After the death of Daniel of Galicia in 1266, the Russians became servile vassals and with the new wealth that commerce brought them, the Mongols began to settle in the cities and even in the countryside, where Berke and Mangku-Temur granted huge estates to their *noyans* and reinforced the feudalism that was to paralyse Russia for the next six hundred years.

When Mangku-Temur died in 1280, he was succeeded by his

brother Tode-Mangku, who became a Sufi and a recluse, and the government was left to his *noyans*. On the west of the Don, Nogai established an almost independent kingdom of his own, which included the vassal kingdom of Bulgaria and contained Rumanians and Cumans among its subjects. Through the other Rumanians who lived in Transylvania and the Cumans who had returned with King Bela IV, his influence extended into Hungary, and it was this that led to the last invasion of Europe. King Bela had welcomed new Cuman immigrants to replace the army that had been lost at Mohi, and to regain their trust after the murder of their khan he had married his son Stephen to a Cuman princess. When Bela died in 1270, Stephen V reigned for only two years and was succeeded by his ten-year-old son Ladislas IV, who, under the influence of his mother, rejected the western ways of his courtiers and became known as 'Ladislas the Cuman'. As he grew older, his resistance to his barons and bishops grew stronger and when they passed a law requiring him to convert his Cumans to Christianity, he arrested the papal legate, imprisoned his Christian wife, Isabel of Anjou, married two Cuman princesses from Nogai's court and went to live in a Cuman camp. The barons raised an army, the Archbishop of Gran preached a crusade and Ladislas turned for help to Nogai. It was the chance that many of the *noyans* had been waiting for. Nogai persuaded the khan's nephew Tole-Buka to join him and in the winter of 1285 the Mongol armies returned to Europe.

From the outset the campaign was no more than ill-conceived and disorganized opportunism and although the commanders attempted to follow the strategies of Subedei, both they and their soldiers lacked the determination and stamina of their pre-decessors. While Nogai occupied Transylvania, where his presence deterred the Hungarian barons from attacking their king, Tole-Buka set out to invade Hungary from the north, but when his army got stuck in the snowdrifts of the Carpathian passes, he turned back to Volynia and allowed his frustrated soldiers to plunder the defenceless towns of their vassals and allies. In the spring of 1286 Nogai withdrew from Transylvania and in the autumn the two armies invaded Poland, ostensibly to prevent the Poles from supporting the Hungarian barons. Nogai advanced against Cracow and Tole-Buka attacked Sandomir, but the Poles had learned by past experience. The garrisons were not tempted to engage the enemy in the field, they remained on their walls and both cities held out against the Mongol assaults. As always the countryside was devastated and other cities were sacked, but in most cases it was only because their governors had been tricked into opening their gates when the Russian princes in the Mongol army promised them an amnesty if they surrendered. The rich soldiers of the Golden Horde had lost their ambition for anything other than easy plunder and without Chinese and Persian artillery, they no longer had the ability to capture a fortified capital. Exasperated and disconcerted they returned to Volynia in 1287 and they never came back. Ladislas was left to his fate and in 1290 he was murdered by two Cuman assassins who had been bought by the barons.

When Nogai's armies withdrew from Poland, the cloud of Mongol terror which had hung over Europe for forty-six years began to lift. The khans of the Golden Horde renewed their war against the Mongol khans of Persia and dynastic and territorial wars broke out between the kings of Europe, but the wars which had brought the Christian and Moslem civilizations to the brink of destruction were over and the men whose ambitions had sustained them were dead. The papacy had mastered the Holy Roman Empire, the crusaders had at last been driven from Palestine and the cataclysmic expansion of the Mongol Empire had ended: in the east it was halted by the sea, in the Middle East it was contained by the Mamluks and in the west it had been abandoned. Subedei, who first planned the Mongol dominion of Europe, died in retirement after the conquest of the Sung and the date of his death is uncertain, but, like Frederick II, Hulegu and King Louis, he did not live to see his purpose fail.

The Mongol threat had woken Europe from its ignorant isolation, but under their new masters from the steppes the Persian and Arabic civilizations began to decline. The vulgar materialism of the Mongols and the bigoted puritanism of the Mamluks inhibited their artists. Even in Cairo, which after the fall of Baghdad became the academic capital of Islam, the Mamluks' dogmatic acceptance of all unexplained phenomena as 'the will of Allah' suppressed the curiosity of their scientists. Yet the teachings of the Moslem mathematicians and their translations of the Greek philosophers had reached Europe through Moslem Spain and, similarly, the works of their artists and scientists had been introduced to Europeans by Frederick II. When these seeds began to flower among a newly inquisitive people, they led to a renaissance. Under the patronage of merchants who had grown rich in eastern trade, scholars and scientists forsook their fear of heresy, artists returned to the classical traditions which had survived the censure of Rome in Constantinople, and in time western Christendom replaced Islam as the cultural centre of the world.

As trade increased and the reports of merchants, missionaries and ambassadors became more numerous, new legends were born and the men who had been seen as the soldiers of the devil became the masters of an empire no less fabulous than the mythical empires of India. Copies of Marco Polo's *Description of the World* were not widely circulated until the end of the fourteenth century and by then the Mongol Empire had already found its way into European literature. In Geoffrey Chaucer's *Canterbury Tales*, 'The Squire's Tale' was set in Sarai and the name of the Tartar king was Cambinskan, which was intended to sound like Chingis Khan. The most popular description of the east, published in 1360, was *The Travels of Sir John Mandeville*, which was as spurious as the letters of Alexander the Great had been. Sir John Mandeville was in fact a French doctor from Liège called Jean de Bourgogne who had never visited the east, and his book was plagiarized from the reports of the papal ambassadors. Through the awe which this book generated and the later misinterpretations of Marco Polo, the Mongols and their Chinese subjects were credited with marvellous scientific achievements and many innovations for which they were not responsible. The process of block printing may have been brought back from the east by some European traveller, but neither the Mongols nor Marco Polo introduced the mariner's compass: experiments in this field were being carried out simultaneously in Europe and Syria as well as in China. The Mongols' only certain innovation was to combine the Moslem and oriental schools of astronomy at the observatory in Maragha and the one science which they introduced, and which Europe was slow to learn, was the hideous science of total war.

Gunpowder, which was first discovered in China, was widely used by the Mongols during the reign of Kubilai Khan, but it was not used during the campaigns in Russia and Europe. Enthusiastic theories to the contrary have all been discredited. Yet as early as 1265–6 the formula for its composition was recorded in Europe by the English Franciscan Roger Bacon in his *Epistola de Secretis Operibus Naturae*. He could not have learned it from the chronicles of the Mongol invasion or the reports of observers and ambassadors since none of them described it. Nor could he have learned it from Marco Polo since Marco was only eleven and had not yet visited China. It is therefore argued that gunpowder was separately discovered in Europe or that it was introduced through Islam where some of the components were described by Abd Allah at the beginning of the thirteenth century. However, Roger Bacon's letter was written from Paris where he lived between 1257 and 1267. At that time William of Rubruck was also in Paris, having obtained permission to return from Acre. The two friars met and much of Friar William's report was incorporated into Roger Bacon's *Opus Majus*, which Bacon acknowledges was done with Friar William's help. If Friar William had discovered the formula for the powder which he must have realized would change the face of war, it is unlikely that he would have included the dangerous information in a report which he knew would be widely read. But he might have passed it on to a fellow Franciscan scholar. Even in Roger Bacon's letter the formula was written in code. It does seem to be an extraordinary coincidence that the first European to record the comparatively complicated composition of gunpowder should have done so shortly after meeting the only man to have visited the capital of the one empire where the substance and its uses were well known. It is possible, therefore, that, although the Mongols themselves did not introduce gunpowder into Europe, the formula was brought back secretly from their capital by William of Rubruck.

Unlike the masters of other great empires, the Mongols contributed little to the civilizations that came after them. They adopted the cultures of their subjects and when their empire disintegrated the world forgot them, but they had altered the course of its history and they had left it scarred. Russia was torn away from Europe, and when the Mongols abandoned it after two hundred years it was feudal and backward. Poland and Hungary were so devastated that they never emerged to play their part in the renaissance that followed in the west. Bulgaria, like Russia, was isolated and then fell to the Ottoman Turks, whom the Mongols had driven out of Khwarizm and who were one day to stand on the banks of the Danube as the Mongols had done. The lands that once nurtured the great civilizations of the Persians were returned to the desert and they have never recovered. Wherever the Mongols rode they left an irretrievably ruined economy and wherever they ruled

they left a petty, self-important aristocracy and an exploited peas-
antry. In some countries their legacy of indigence and oppression
survived for centuries until the desperate peoples resorted to
revolution and communism.

The campaigns of the Mongol armies were the last and the most
destructive in the long line of nomad invasions from the steppes. In
just over fifty years they conquered half the known world and it
was only their adherence to tribal traditions and the rivalry of their
princes that denied them the rest of it. Western Europe and Islam
were not saved outside the walls of Cracow and on the field at Ain
Jalut, they were saved before when the Mongol armies halted in
their moment of triumph. If Ogedei and Mangku had not died
when they did, the largest empire that the world had ever known
would have been bounded in the west not by the Carpathians and
the Euphrates, but by the Atlantic Ocean.

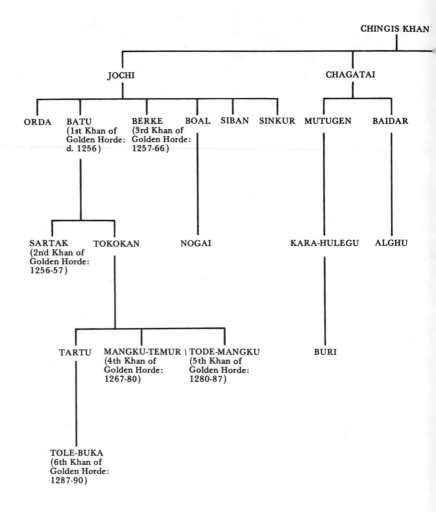

CHINGIS KHAN

JOCHI

CHAGATAI

ORDA BATU
(1st Khan of
Golden Horde:
d. 1256)

BERKE
(3rd Khan of
Golden Horde:
1257-66)

BOAL SIBAN SINKUR MUTUGEN

BAIDAR

SARTAK
(2nd Khan of
Golden Horde:
1256-57)

TOKOKAN

NOGAI

KARA-HULEGU

ALGHU

TARTU

MANGKU-TEMUR | TODE-MANGKU
(4th Khan of
Golden Horde:
1267-80)

(5th Khan of
Golden Horde:
1280-87)

BURI

TOLE-BUKA
(6th Khan of
Golden Horde:
1287-90)

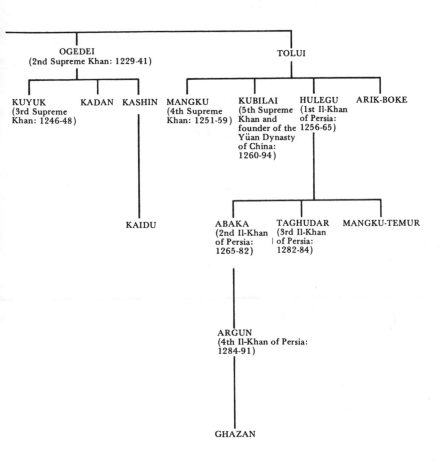

OGEDEI
(2nd Supreme Khan: 1229-41)

TOLUI

KUYUK
(3rd Supreme
Khan: 1246-48)

KADAN   KASHIN

MANGKU
(4th Supreme
Khan: 1251-59)

KUBILAI
(5th Supreme
Khan and
founder of the
Yüan Dynasty
of China:
1260-94)

HULEGU
(1st Il-Khan
of Persia:
1256-65)

ARIK-BOKE

KAIDU

ABAKA
(2nd Il-Khan
of Persia:
1265-82)

TAGHUDAR
(3rd Il-Khan
of Persia:
1282-84)

MANGKU-TEMUR

ARGUN
(4th Il-Khan of Persia:
1284-91)

GHAZAN

Select Bibliography

I PRIMARY SOURCES

The Secret History of the Mongols
The original Mongol text has not survived, but it was translated into Chinese under the Ming Dynasty in 1382. German translation by E. Haenisch, *Die geheime Geschichte der Mongolen* (Leipzig 1948). Extensively annotated but incomplete French translation by P. Pelliot, *Histoire Secrète des Mongols* (Paris 1949). English excerpts translated by A.Waley, *The Secret History of the Mongols and other Pieces* (London 1963).

Ssanang Setzen, *The Precious Summary*
Seventeenth-century chronicle by the Prince of Ordos. German translation by I.J. Schmidt, *Geschichte der Ost-Mongolen* (St Petersburg 1829). Incomplete English translation by J.R. Krueger, *A History of the Eastern Mongols to 1662* (Bloomington, Indiana 1964).

The Campaigns of Chingis Khan
Chinese History compiled during the reign of Kubilai Khan. French translation by P. Pelliot and L. Hambis, *Histoire des Campagnes de Genghis Khan* (Leiden 1951).

E. Bretschneider, *Medieval Researches from Eastern Asiatic Sources* (London 1888, reprinted 1967)
English translations of contemporary Chinese records.

Juvaini, *History of the World Conqueror*
Contemporary Persian history. English translation by J.A. Boyle (Manchester 1958).

Rashid ad-Din, *Compendium of Histories*
Contemporary Persian history by a vizier who was executed in 1318. French translation of the history of the reign of Hulegu by

E. Quatremère, *Histoire des Mongols de la Perse* (Paris 1836, reprinted 1968).

Bar Hebraeus, *Chronography*
Contemporary Syriac record by the Jacobite Christian prelate who lived in Maragha. English translation by W. Bridges (Oxford 1932).

Gregory of Akner, *A History of the Nation of Archers*
Contemporary Armenian history. English translation by R.P. Blake and R.N. Frye (Cambridge, Mass. 1954).

Hayton the Monk, *La Flor des Estoires de la Terre d'Orient*
Written in French and Latin by the nephew of the King of Little Armenia who lived in France. Texts published in *Recueil des Historiens des Croisades. Documents Arméniens* (1906).

The Georgian Chronicle
French translation by M. Brosset, *Histoire de la Georgie*, 4 vols (St Petersburg 1849–58, reprinted 1969).

The Chronicle of Novgorod
English translation by R. Mitchell and N. Forbes (London 1914).

Polnoe Sobranie Russkikh Letopisei, Vol. 10 (St Petersburg 1885)
Complete Collection of Russian Chronicles. English translation of passages relating to the Mongol conquest by B. Dmytryshyn, *Medieval Russia* (Hinsdale, Illinois 1973).

Monumenta Germaniae Historica (Hanover and Berlin 1826 *et seq.* several reprints)
This collection contains the Latin texts of many of the contemporary central European reports and chronicles.

Simon of Saint Quentin, *Historia Tartarorum*
This was a major source for Vincent of Beauvais' *Speculum Historiale* (Douai 1624 and reprints) French edition by J. Richard, *Simon de Saint Quentin, Histoire des Tartares* (Paris 1965).

John of Plano Carpini, *Itinerarium et Historia Mongolorum*
Benedict the Pole, *De Itinere ad Tartaros*
William of Rubruck, *Itinerarium ad Partes Orientales*
English translations by W.W. Rockhill in *The Journey of William of Rubruck to the Eastern Parts of the World, 1253–55, as Narrated by Himself with Two Accounts of The Earlier Journey of John of Pian de*

Carpine (London 1900). Quotations in this book are taken from the translation by a nun of Stanbrook Abbey, edited and introduced by Christopher Dawson in *The Mongol Mission* (London 1955). A longer version of Friar Benedict's record, believed to have been written by a brother monk, is printed with an English translation in R.A. Skelton, T.E. Marston and G.D. Painter's *The Vinland Map and the Tartar Relation* (New Haven 1965).

Matthew Paris, *Chronica Majora*
A history of England during the reign of Henry III which also covers events in Europe including the Mongol invasion and records many of the contemporary letters and documents. English translation by J.A. Giles (London 1852–4 and reprints).

Sir H. Yule and H. Cordier (ed.), *The Book of Ser Marco Polo the Venetian Concerning the Kingdoms and Marvels of the East* (London 1903, reprint 1963).

2 SECONDARY SOURCES

W.E.D. Allen, *A History of the Georgian People* (London 1932).
V.V. Barthold, *Turkestan down to the Mongol Invasion*, Eng. trans. H.A.R. Gibb (London 1968).
W. Blunt, *The Golden Road to Samarkand* (London 1973).
S. Bökönyi, *The Przevalsky Horse*, Eng. trans. L. Halápy (London 1974).
J. Boudet (ed.), *The Ancient Art of Warfare* (London 1966).
L. Bréhier, *L'Eglise et l'Orient au Moyen Age* (Paris 1921).
P. Brent, *The Mongol Empire* (London 1976).
E.G. Browne, *A Literary History of Persia*, Vols 2 and 3 (Cambridge 1902–24).
J. Bryce, *The Holy Roman Empire* (London 1906).
Cambridge History of Poland, Vol. 1 (1950).
Cambridge Medieval History Vol. 4 (1966) and Vol. 6 (1968).
Cambridge History of Islam, Vol. 1 (1970).
Cambridge History of Iran, Vol. 5 (1968).
J.D. Clarkson, *A History of Russia* (New York 1961).
C. Commeaux, *La Vie Quotidienne chez les Mongols de la Conquête* (Paris 1972).
J. Curtin, *The Mongols in Russia* (Boston 1908).
I. de Rachewiltz, *Papal Envoys to the Great Khans* (London 1971).
M. d'Ohsson, *Histoire des Mongols depuis Tchinguiz-Khan jusqu'à Timour Bey* (Amsterdam 1852).

T.N. Dupuy, *The Military Life of Genghis: Khan of Khans* (New York 1969).

J.F.C. Fuller, *Decisive Battles of the Western World* (London 1954).

R. Fox, *Genghis Khan* (London 1936).

J.B. Glubb, *Soldiers of Fortune; the Story of the Mamluks* (London 1973)
—— *The Lost Centuries* (London 1967).

B. Grekov and A. Iakoubovski, *La Horde d'Or et la Russie* (Paris 1961).

R. Grousset, *Conqueror of the World*, Eng. trans. D. Sinor and M. MacKellar (London 1967).
—— *L'Empire des Steppes* (Paris 1969).

E.G. Heath, *The Grey Goose Wing* (Reading 1971).

H. Howorth, *History of the Mongols* (London 1876, reprint 1965).

M. Jankovich, *They Rode into Europe*, Eng. trans. A. Dent (London 1971).

E.H. Kantorowicz, *Frederick the Second*, Eng. trans. E.O. Lorimer (London 1931).

S. Lane Poole, *Egypt in the Middle Ages* (London 1901).

H. Lamb, *Genghis Khan: The Emperor of All Men* (New York 1928).

D.M. Lang, *The Bulgarians: From Pagan Times to the Ottoman Conquest* (London 1976).

J.D. Latham and W.F. Paterson, trans. and ed., *Saracen Archery* (London 1970).

A.W.A. Leeper, *A History of Medieval Austria* (Oxford 1941).

S. Legg, *The Heartland* (London 1970).

M. Letts, *Mandeville's Travels: Texts and Translations* (London 1953).

B.H. Liddell Hart, *Great Captains Unveiled* (London 1927).

H.D. Martin, *The Rise of Chingis Khan and his Conquest of North China* (Baltimore 1950).

A.C. Moule, *Christians in China before 1550* (London 1930).

W. Muir, *The Mameluke or Slave Dynasty of Egypt* (London 1896, reprint 1968).

L. Olschki, *Marco Polo's Asia*, Eng. trans. J.A. Scott (Los Angeles 1960)

C.W.C. Oman, *The Art of War in the Middle Ages* (Oxford 1885, reprint 1968).

E. Pamlenyi (ed.), *A History of Hungary*, Eng. trans. (Budapest 1973).

R. Payne-Gallwey, *The Crossbow with a treatise and appendix on the Catapult, the Balista and the Turkish Bow* (London 1907).

P. Pelliot, *Notes sur l'histoire de la Horde d'Or par Bertold Spuler* (Paris 1950).
—— *Notes sur Marco Polo*, 2 Vols (Paris 1959–63).
—— 'Les Mongols et la Papaute', *Revue de l'Orient Chrétien*, Vol. 23, pp. 1–28 (1922); Vol. 24, pp. 225–335 (1924); Vol. 28, pp. 3–84 (1931).

M. Percheron, *Les Conquérants d'Asie* (Paris 1951).

E.D. Phillips, *The Mongols* (London 1969).

S. Runciman, *A History of the Crusades*, Vol. 3 (Cambridge 1955).

J.J. Saunders, *The History of the Mongol Conquests* (London 1971).

F. Schevill, *History of the Balkan Peninsula: From Earliest Times to the Present Day* (New York 1922, reprint 1966).

R.W. Seton-Watson, *A History of the Czechs and Slovaks* (London 1943).

D. Seward, *The Monks of War* (London 1972).

E. Sheppard, 'Military Methods of the Mongols', *Army Quarterly*, Vol. 18, pp. 305–15 (USA 1929).

D. Sinor, *A History of Hungary* (London 1957).

—— *Introduction à l'étude de l'Eurasie Centrale* (Wiesbaden 1963).

B. Spuler, *History of the Mongols based on Eastern and Western Accounts of the thirteenth and fourteenth century*, Eng. trans. H. and S. Drummond (London 1972).

—— *The Mongols in History*, Eng. trans. G. Wheeler (London 1971).

—— *Die Golden Horde. Die Mongolen in Russland* (Wiesbaden 1965).

—— *Die Mongolen in Iran* (Berlin 1968).

G. Strakosch-Grassmann, *Der Einfall der Mongolen in Mitteleuropa* (Innsbruck 1893).

G. Vernadsky, *Kievan Russia* (New Haven 1948).

—— *The Mongols and Russia* (New Haven 1953).

B.J. Vladimirtsov, *Le Régime Social des Mongols. Le Féodalisme Nomade*, Fr. trans. M. Carsow (Paris 1948).

—— *Life of Chingis Khan*, Eng. trans. D.S. Mirsky (New York 1930).

H. Yule, *Cathay and the Way Thither*, 4 Vols (London 1913–16).

Glossary

Arban Mongol troop of ten men.
Atabeg Turkish governor: literally father governor.
Bahadur Mongol knight: literally hero.
Bezant European coin originally struck in Byzantium.
Boyar Russian baron.
Brodniki Community of nomad fishermen on the Lower Don.
Caliph Moslem religious ruler: literally successor (to the Prophet).
Cumans Turko-Mongol nomads of the Russian steppes.
Gurkhan Turkish ruler of Kara Khitai.
Il-khan Mongol ruler of Persia, subordinate to the supreme khan.
Imam Eminent Moslem who leads the congregation in prayer.
Jacobites Dissident Christian sect founded by Jacobus Baradaeus.
Jagun Mongol squadron of 100 men.
Kalat Mongol tunic.
Kanglis Tribe of Cumans.
Kashik Mongol imperial guard.
Kipchaks Eastern name for Cumans.
Kumiz Alcoholic drink made from fermented mares' milk.
Mamluks Slave soldiers who became rulers of Egypt.
Mangudai Mongol unit which feigned flight to tempt its enemy into an
  ambush.
Minghan Mongol regiment of 1,000 men.
Musalla Open place where Moslem salat (ritual prayer) is performed on
  special occasions.
Naccara Mongol kettle drum.
Naphtha Inflammable oil.
Nestorians Dissident Christian sect founded by Nestorius.
Noyan Mongol baron and military commander of 1,000 or more.
Ordu Mongol camp.
Orlok Mongol field marshal.
Paitze Mongol tablet of authority.
Saracens Greek and Roman name for Syrio-Arabian nomads. Later
  used by Crusaders to describe Moslems.

Seljuks Moslem Turks; xith century conquerors of eastern Islam and xiiith century rulers of Rum.

Shamanism Primitive Ural-Altaic religion: belief in good and evil spirits.

Taoism Ancient, philosophical Chinese religion.

Tulughma Mongol manoeuvre – the standard sweep.

Tumen Mongol division of 10,000 men.

Vizier Senior Moslem minister.

Yam Mongol post system.

Yurt Mongol tent.

Yurtchi Mongol quartermaster.

Index